READING AND VOCABULARY 2

Focus

Deborah Gordon and **Laurie Blass**

Series Consultant
Lawrence J. Zwier

NATIONAL GEOGRAPHIC LEARNING | CENGAGE Learning

Australia • Brazil • Japan • Korea • Mexico • Singapore • Spain • United Kingdom • United States

Reading and Vocabulary Focus 2
Deborah Gordon and Laurie Blass

Publisher: Sherrise Roehr

Series Consultant: Lawrence J. Zwier

Executive Editor: Laura Le Dréan

Contributing Editors: Bernard Seal and
Jennifer Bixby

Director of Global Marketing: Ian Martin

International Marketing Manager: Caitlin Thomas

Director, Content and Media Production:
Michael Burggren

Senior Content Project Manager: Daisy Sosa

Print Buyer: Mary Beth Hennebury

Cover Designers: Christopher Roy and
Michael Rosenquest

Cover Image: Greg Dale/National Geographic
Creative

Text Design and Layout: Don Williams

Composition: Page Designs International

For product information and technology assistance, contact us at
**Cengage Learning Customer & Sales Support,
1-800-354-9706**
For permission to use material from this text or product,
submit all requests online at **www.cengage.com/permissions**.
Further permissions questions can be e-mailed to
permissionrequest@cengage.com.

Student Book ISBN: 978-1-285-17331-3

National Geographic Learning
20 Channel Center Street
Boston, MA 02210
USA

Cengage Learning is a leading provider of customized learning solutions with office locations around the globe, including Singapore, the United Kingdom, Australia, Mexico, Brazil and Japan.

Cengage Learning products are represented in Canada by Nelson Education, Ltd.

Visit National Geographic Learning online at **ngl.cengage.com**

Visit our corporate website at **www.cengage.com**

Printed in the United States of America
3 4 5 6 7 8   19 18 17 16 15 14

CONTENTS

FOOD

ONE

THE FACE

TWO

CITIES

THREE

CONTENTS (CONTINUED)

FOUR

FIVE

SIX

SEVEN

EIGHT

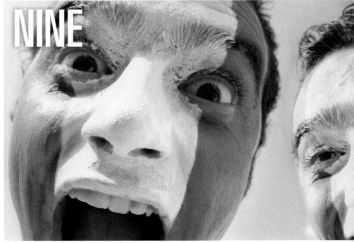

NINE

INSIDE A UNIT

Each unit opens with an amazing **National Geographic** image that taps into learners' natural curiosity about the world while introducing the content that will be explored in the readings.

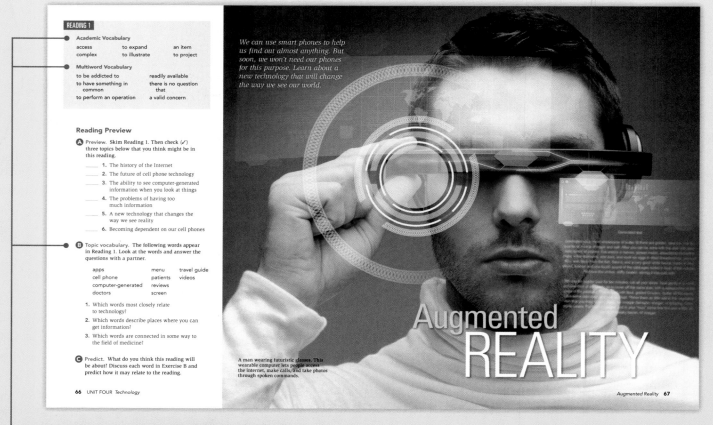

A comprehensive, three-part **vocabulary development program** builds student confidence as learners meet new or unfamiliar words in academic texts.

READING 1 AUGMENTED REALITY

You've just arrived at a party, but you don't see anyone you know. Who should you talk to? You put on a special pair of glasses and look at the people again. Now, when you look around, you see information about each person on their faces or chests. You see the job each person has. You also see each person's interests. You can even see the friends you have in common. As you look around, you notice someone who knows several of your friends, likes the same kind of music as you, and also loves to cook. You approach this person.

"Augmented reality, or AR, adds pictures, sounds, text, and other types of information to the real world."

Can you buy these special glasses right now? No, not quite yet. But a technology called *augmented reality* may make them readily available soon. What is augmented reality? *Augment* means to "add to something or expand something." So, augmented reality is an expanded reality. Augmented reality, or AR, adds pictures, sounds, text, and other types of information to the real world. This extra information comes from computer software.

Some forms of AR are already in use. You can see them on television. For example, when you watch a sport such as soccer, you can see the score and the amount of playing time on the TV screen. In addition, the TV producers often draw circles or lines on the TV screen to more clearly illustrate something. This is a simple kind of AR that has been around for many years. Doctors use a more complex type of AR. For example, they can project an MRI[1] scan of a person's head onto the head itself. Then, while they are performing an operation, the doctors can look at the MRI scan on the patient's head. Doctors can also project videos of complicated operations onto their patients' bodies. The video shows them what to do next.

AR is not just for television, doctors, or other professionals. Many AR applications—software

[1] *MRI (magnetic resonance imaging):* a picture of the soft parts inside a person's body

programs—already exist for smartphones. Smartphone AR uses your phone's GPS software, so it knows where you are. Based on your location, the application, or app, can connect to and then show you information about nearby places and objects that have already been entered into a database. For example, imagine you're walking down the street trying to decide where to eat. There's an application for that. Just hold your phone up to a street with restaurants and your phone will show you reviews, menu items, and prices—already entered into a database—in front of the restaurants you see. Have you ever lost your car in a parking lot? There's an AR app for that! Just get out of your car and take a picture. Later, the AR application on your phone will use GPS to direct you back to your car. Are you interested in the stars? Hold your phone up to the sky. You will see the names of the stars. You can also see the names of the constellations.[2] There's an app for that, too.

Many other useful AR apps are already in use on smartphones. Travelers can use AR apps instead of carrying around a guidebook or hiring

[2] *constellations:* groups of stars that form a pattern

a travel guide. When you are traveling, just point your phone at something to get information about it. For example, point your phone at the Eiffel Tower and read its height, age, and admission price on the screen. There are AR apps for shoppers, too. Point your phone at an item in a store, for example, and get information on the price and quality. You can even get information on the same product at other stores.

In the future, we probably won't use cell phone screens to see augmented reality. A pair of glasses or contact lenses[3] might be all we need. This is an exciting idea, but there are some concerns. Some people worry that AR might produce too much information. Sometimes, too much information can be confusing. Others worry that people might get to be addicted to seeing reality through AR apps. They think people might come to prefer augmented reality to actual reality. These may be valid concerns. However, there is no question that AR is here to stay. Soon, everyone will have access to it and people will learn to get used to it.

[3] *contact lenses:* small plastic lenses that go on the surface of the eyes to improve eyesight

68 UNIT FOUR Technology

Augmented Reality 69

Content-rich readings supported by real-world images, maps, charts, and informational graphics prepare learners for academic success.

After each reading . . .

READING COMPREHENSION

Big Picture

A Below are the topics of each paragraph in Reading 1. Number them in the order in which they appear in the reading.

_____ a. An explanation of the meaning of the term *augmented reality*

_____ b. The possible future of augmented reality

_____ c. Current uses of augmented reality for tourists and shoppers

_____ d. An example of a person using augmented reality at a party

_____ e. Current uses of augmented reality on TV and in hospitals

_____ f. Current uses of augmented reality on smartphones

B Compare answers to Exercise A with a partner. Then discuss what you think the main idea of the whole reading is.

Close-Up

A Choose the word or phrase in parentheses that correctly completes each sentence.

1. According to the reading, what happens at the party in paragraph 1 (is / is not) possible now.

2. According to paragraph 2, augmented reality allows you to see (information about / what's inside) the things in front of you.

3. According to paragraph 3, television producers already use augmented reality for (drama / sports) programs.

4. Doctors are (already / not yet) able to see projected videos on their patients.

5. According to paragraph 4, smartphone-based AR (needs / does not need) to know your location in order to work.

6. According to paragraphs 4 and 5, smartphone applications use augmented reality for (mainly practical / mainly entertainment) purposes already.

7. Augmented reality applications on smartphones (can already / cannot yet) replace guidebooks for tourists and travelers.

8. So far, most personal use of augmented reality is only (through special glasses / on a smartphone screen).

9. Some people wonder if augmented reality will cause problems because (people might use it too often / it might be bad for your eyes).

10. According to the reading, we (will / will not) probably all have access to augmented reality very soon.

B Compare answers to Exercise A with a partner. If you don't agree, find statements in Reading 1 that support your answers.

70 UNIT FOUR Technology

Reading Comprehension sections assess learner comprehension through a variety of activities.

Learners are taught an essential **reading skill** and then apply that skill meaningfully to the reading.

Reading Skill

Connecting Examples to the Main Ideas They Support

Writers often use examples to support their main ideas. Examples help the reader to understand the main points a writer is trying to make. Writers often signal that they are providing an example to support a main idea by using signal words and phrases. These include *for example*, *such as*, *for instance*, and *like*. Good readers look for these signal words and phrases to help them find examples so they can better understand the main ideas of a reading.

Notice how the example below helps to clarify the writer's main idea.

Some forms of AR are already in use. You can see them on television. For example, when you watch a sport such as soccer, you can see the score . . .

In the sentence above, *For example* signals the example. However, not all example sentences use signal words. Notice how there are no signal words in the second sentence below to show that it is providing a supporting example for the main idea before it.

Many other useful AR applications are already in use on smartphones. Travelers can use AR applications instead of carrying around a guidebook or hiring a travel guide.

A Read the examples in the chart below. Find the missing ideas the examples support in Reading 1. Write the main ideas in the chart.

Main Ideas	Examples
1. *You see information about each person on their faces or chests.*	You see the job each person has. (Par. 1)
2.	For example, they [doctors] can project an MRI scan of a person's head onto the head itself. (Par. 3)
3.	Just get out of your car and take a picture. Later, the AR application on your phone will use GPS to direct you back to your car. (Par. 4)
4.	For example, point your phone at the Eiffel Tower and read its height, age, and admission price on the screen. (Par. 5)
5.	Point your phone at an item in a store, for example, and get information on the price and quality. (Par. 5)

Academic Vocabulary sections develop the language that students are likely to encounter in authentic academic readings.

VOCABULARY PRACTICE

Academic Vocabulary

A Find the words in bold in Reading 1. Use the context to help you choose the definition that is closest to the meaning in the reading.

1. **expand** (Par. 2)
   a. grow in size
   b. give more information on
2. **illustrate** (Par. 3)
   a. draw
   b. show
3. **complex** (Par. 3)
   a. difficult to understand
   b. advanced technologically
4. **project** (Par. 3)
   a. stick out of
   b. make something appear
5. **items** (Par. 4)
   a. objects such as food
   b. topics
6. **access** (Par. 6)
   a. opportunity to use
   b. a way to enter

B Choose an academic word from Exercise A to complete each of the following sentences. Notice and learn the words in bold because they often appear with the academic words.

1. The Sherwood Diner is a small restaurant, but all the **menu** _____ are delicious.
2. The surgeons could not _____ **the video** of the operation onto the patient's chest.
3. You can't see all the different parts of that Web site for free. You need to have a password to **get** _____ to some parts.
4. Laser tag is a _____ **form** of the simple children's game of tag most of us played when we were young.
5. Good photographs can help to **clearly** _____ the more complicated parts of a presentation.
6. Smartphones can _____ our **reality** by giving us useful facts about the things around us.

Multiword Vocabulary

A Find the multiword vocabulary in bold in Reading 1. Use the context to help you understand the meaning. Then match each item to the correct definition.

_____ 1. **have in common** (Par. 1)
_____ 2. **readily available** (Par. 2)
_____ 3. **performing an operation** (Par. 3)
_____ 4. **be addicted to** (Par. 6)
_____ 5. **valid concerns** (Par. 6)
_____ 6. **there is no question that** (Par. 6)

a. it is certain that
b. easy to buy or get
c. unable to stop doing something
d. things that are serious and important enough to worry about
e. share with
f. cutting into someone's body to fix a medical condition

B Complete the following sentences with the correct multiword vocabulary from Exercise A.

1. Teens often don't get as much sleep as they need. Parents who worry about this have _____ because studies show that not getting enough sleep can lead to health problems.
2. People who cannot stop themselves from surfing the Internet when they should be doing other things may _____ the Internet.
3. My parents have been happily married for 50 years. The secret to their success is that they _____ their love of gardening.
4. Professor Walker strongly emphasizes assignments. Class participation may or may not affect your grade. _____ that students who do no homework will fail the class.
5. Many people believe that full-size electric cars will soon be more affordable and _____ to all drivers.
6. Medical students often get nervous the first time they are _____ on a patient.

Use the Vocabulary

Write the following lists. Then share your lists with a partner and talk about why you chose the items on your lists.

Make a list of the following:
- Three things that people can **be addicted to**
- Three things that you and a good friend of yours **have in common**
- Three things about learning English that begin: "For me, **there is no question that** . . ."
- Three public places you know of where you can get free **access** to the Internet
- Three **valid concerns** that parents of teenage children often have
- Three **items** of clothing that you have in your closet that you never use
- Three **complex relationships** that you have with friends or members of your family

In **Use the Vocabulary**, students get to activate the newly-learned vocabulary in new and interesting contexts.

Multiword Vocabulary sections identify words that are commonly grouped together and then prompt learners to work with them in different contexts for enhanced comprehension.

VOCABULARY INDEX

The following words and phrases are studied in *Reading and Vocabulary Focus 2*. Each vocabulary item is listed according to which unit and reading it appears in. For example, a word or phrase listed as U1 R1 appears in the first reading of unit 1. If a word is in the Academic Word List, it is listed as ███.

For easy reference, a **Vocabulary Index** in the back of every student book lists all the academic and multiword vocabulary from the lessons.

THINK AND DISCUSS

Work in a small group. Use the information in the reading and your own ideas to discuss the following questions.

1. **Summarize.** According to Reading 1, what aspects of augmented reality could cause valid concerns?

2. **Apply knowledge.** Which would you prefer to use when traveling—augmented reality glasses or information from a guidebook or a Web site? If you would like to use both, when would you use the glasses and when would you use a book or Web site?

3. **Express an opinion.** According to Reading 1, we may all one day have special AR glasses that let us see information about people and things when we look at them. What information would you not want people to see about you?

Augmented Reality **73**

Think and Discuss questions at the end of each reading require learners to discuss their opinions on the topic while making connections to their own lives.

The **Vocabulary Review** recycles the key vocabulary from the unit and offers meaningful, contextualized practice opportunities.

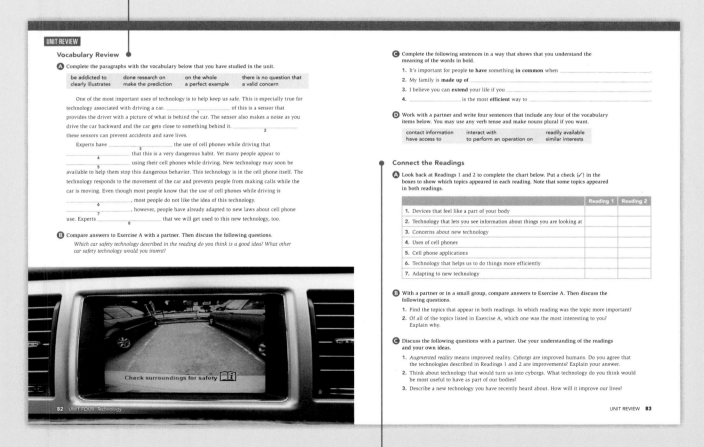

UNIT REVIEW

Vocabulary Review

A Complete the paragraphs with the vocabulary below that you have studied in the unit.

| be addicted to | done research on | on the whole | there is no question that |
| clearly illustrates | make the prediction | a perfect example | a valid concern |

One of the most important uses of technology is to help keep us safe. This is especially true for technology associated with driving a car. _____1_____ of this is a sensor that provides the driver with a picture of what is behind the car. The sensor also makes a noise as you drive the car backward and the car gets close to something behind it. _____2_____ these sensors can prevent accidents and save lives.

Experts have _____3_____ the use of cell phones while driving that _____4_____ that this is a very dangerous habit. Yet many people appear to _____5_____ using their cell phones while driving. New technology may soon be available to help them stop this dangerous behavior. This technology is in the cell phone itself. The technology responds to the movement of the car and prevents people from making calls while the car is moving. Even though most people know that the use of cell phones while driving is _____6_____, most people do not like the idea of this technology. _____7_____, however, people have already adapted to new laws about cell phone use. Experts _____8_____ that we will get used to this new technology, too.

B Compare answers to Exercise A with a partner. Then discuss the following questions.
Which car safety technology described in the reading do you think is a good idea? What other car safety technology would you invent?

Check surroundings for safety

82 UNIT FOUR *Technology*

C Complete the following sentences in a way that shows that you understand the meaning of the words in bold.

1. It's important for people **to have** something **in common** when _____.

2. My family is **made up of** _____.

3. I believe you can **extend** your life if you _____.

4. _____ is the most **efficient** way to _____.

D Work with a partner and write four sentences that include any four of the vocabulary items below. You may use any verb tense and make nouns plural if you want.

| contact information | interact with | readily available |
| have access to | to perform an operation on | similar interests |

Connect the Readings

A Look back at Readings 1 and 2 to complete the chart below. Put a check (✓) in the boxes to show which topics appeared in each reading. Note that some topics appeared in both readings.

	Reading 1	Reading 2
1. Devices that feel like a part of your body		
2. Technology that lets you see information about things you are looking at		
3. Concerns about new technology		
4. Uses of cell phones		
5. Cell phone applications		
6. Technology that helps us to do things more efficiently		
7. Adapting to new technology		

B With a partner or in a small group, compare answers to Exercise A. Then discuss the following questions.

1. Find the topics that appear in both readings. In which reading was the topic more important?

2. Of all of the topics listed in Exercise A, which one was the most interesting to you? Explain why.

C Discuss the following questions with a partner. Use your understanding of the readings and your own ideas.

1. *Augmented reality* means improved reality. *Cyborgs* are improved humans. Do you agree that the technologies described in Readings 1 and 2 are improvements? Explain your answer.

2. Think about technology that would turn us into cyborgs. What technology do you think would be most useful to have as part of our bodies?

3. Describe a new technology you have recently heard about. How will it improve our lives?

UNIT REVIEW **83**

Connect the Readings sections at the end of each unit practice critical thinking skills as learners are guided to compare, contrast, and synthesize information from the two readings.

SERIES INTRODUCTION

Welcome to National Geographic Learning's new Reading and Vocabulary Focus *series. The series delivers memorable reading experiences, develops essential reading skills, and showcases a wide variety of high-utility vocabulary. The passages take readers to exciting new places where they can apply the skills of successful academic readers. While engaged with the content, readers encounter target vocabulary that is ample, diverse, and presented with a fresh, pragmatic view of what the term vocabulary item truly means.*

Great reading classes depend on top-of-the-line content. That's why we've taken such great care in selecting content for *Reading and Vocabulary Focus*. Through all four levels (high beginning to low advanced), *Reading and Vocabulary Focus* draws from the vast resources of National Geographic. High-interest reading content written by some of the world's most authoritative and thought-provoking reporters and explorers is presented in level-appropriate language and used to build reading skills and to promote vocabulary learning. Skill building is of course important, but not for its own sake. Our goal is always, first and foremost, for students to enjoy working with readings that are truly interesting and worth reading.

A BROADBAND APPROACH TO VOCABULARY

A distinctive feature of *Focus* is its broadband approach to vocabulary. For each reading passage, three groups of vocabulary are called out:

1) 10–12 topic-related vocabulary items to consider in pre-reading activities
2) 6–8 academic words—single word items essential to building an academic vocabulary
3) 6–8 multiword vocabulary items useful in academic reading

A systematic focus on multiword vocabulary sets *Reading and Vocabulary Focus* apart from most reading/vocabulary texts. Increasingly, more and more teachers and many textbooks recognize that some vocabulary items consist of more than one word, especially phrasal/prepositional verbs (*hurry up, take on*) and compound nouns (*glass ceiling, weather station*). However, the amount of effort and text space devoted to expanding students' multiword repertoires is typically minimal and the approach haphazard.

Our thinking in the *Reading and Vocabulary Focus* series has been influenced by numerous researchers who have examined the great importance to native speakers of conventionalized multi-word units, whether those units are called "chunks," "strings," or something else. Schmitt and Carter settle on the term *formulaic sequences* and point out a helpful description by Wray, that formulaic sequences "are stored and retrieved whole from memory at the time of use rather than being subject to generation and analysis at the time of use by the language grammar." (Schmitt & Carter, 2012, 13)[1]

It is not always easy to decide whether a group of words constitutes a unit so tight and useful that it should be taught as a discrete vocabulary item. In our item selection for *Focus*, we applied the criterion of "stored and retrieved whole." An item could make the cut if, in the expert judgment of our authors and editors, it was probably treated cognitively as a whole thing. In this way, we were able to judge that such diverse language as *pay attention to*, *on the whole*, *an invasion of privacy*, and *be the first to admit* are formulaic sequences that learners should study and learn as whole units. We checked our judgment against as many sources as possible, including corpora such as the Bank of English (part of the Collins COBUILD corpus) and the online version of the *Corpus of Contemporary American English* (COCA).[2]

UNIT STRUCTURE

Each unit of *Reading and Vocabulary Focus* begins with a high-impact photograph related to the unit theme to capture the students' imaginations and allow for pre-reading discussion. The unit theme encourages inquiry and exploration and offers opportunities for synthesis of information. Two reading passages, related to each other thematically, form the heart of the unit. Each reading is followed by stages of comprehension work, reading skill practice, formative vocabulary exercises, and discussion. Finally the unit ends with a comprehensive vocabulary review section and critical thinking synthesizing tasks.

Pre-Reading and Reading

For each reading passage, pre-reading activities include a task that activates content schemata and a vocabulary exercise that provides a set of clues to the content that the reader will encounter while reading. Each reading has been chosen for high-interest and conceptual challenge and is presented in the company of some of the world's most stimulating photography and other graphics.

Comprehension and Vocabulary Development

Comprehension exercises after each reading start out with a focus on main ideas ("Big Picture") and move to details ("Close-Up"). Then a concise treatment of a high-utility reading skill leads into practice of the skill applied to the reading passage. The vocabulary section after each reading proceeds from the broadband approach mentioned earlier. First come exercises in recognizing

---

[1] Norbert Schmitt and Ronald Carter, Introduction to Formulaic Sequences: Acquisition, Processing, and Use, in Norbert Schmitt, ed. (2004), *Formulaic Sequences: Acquisition, Processing, and Use*, John Benjamins.

[2] At corpus.byu.edu/coca/

academic words and placing them in context. Many of the items in this section are from the Academic Word List (AWL); whether from the AWL or not, every "academic word" is important in academic discourse. Then comes a section of multiword vocabulary, focusing on formulaic sequences as described earlier in this introduction.

Discussion

After studying the vocabulary, students are prompted to use it in discussion activities. Finally, Think and Discuss questions at the end of each reading prompt learners to discuss their opinions on the topic of the reading while making connections to their own lives.

Unit Review

The *Unit Review* consists of two parts: Vocabulary Review and Connect the Readings. The first section of the vocabulary review draws together vocabulary of all types into a richly contextualized exercise. Learners then encounter and practice the vocabulary from the unit, strengthening semantic networks and integrating a wide variety of items into their repertoires. The second section of the unit review, Connect the Readings, takes students' critical-thinking skills to a very high level as they analyze both readings and discover similarities/differences, agreement/disagreement, and other concept relationships.

Reading and Vocabulary Focus has been conceived to respect the wide-ranging curiosity and critical-thinking power of contemporary students. Every day these readers encounter a flood of information. They face unprecedented demands to sort the significant from the trivial and to synthesize information. We are delighted to help them do this by offering great readings, engaging skills development, and top-tier vocabulary learning all in an inviting, visually striking form.

Lawrence J. Zwier
Series Consultant

Child carrying harvested
maize, Madagascar

FOOD

FOCUS

1. What food do you like the most? What food do you like the least?

2. How important is food to you? Do you eat to live, or do you live to eat?

3

Academic Vocabulary

contemporary	an instrument	a structure
to explore	a material	

Multiword Vocabulary

to end up as	to range from . . . to
not surprisingly	to take the place of
nothing more than	to throw away

Reading Preview

A **Preview.** Read the title of Reading 1. Look at the photos on pages 4–8 and read their captions. Then discuss the following questions with a partner or in a small group.

1. What objects do you see in the photos?

2. What do you think the objects are made of?

3. What are some possible uses for food besides eating?

B **Topic vocabulary.** The following words appear in Reading 1. Look at the words and answer the questions with a partner.

carving	flute	radishes
concrete	horns	sculpture
cutting	mushroom	watermelon
drum	pumpkins	

1. Which words are musical instruments?

2. Which words are types of food?

3. Which words are related to making things?

C **Predict.** What do you think this reading will be about? Discuss each word in Exercise B and predict how it may relate to the reading.

Vegetables with eyes added to them look down on little toy people.

Food is only for eating, right? Well, no—not always. Read about some other fascinating uses for the things that we normally eat.

Foods
with
Many
Uses

W hen most people think about
chocolate, cheese, and vegetables,
they think about good things to eat.
However, some very creative people are finding
unexpected uses for food that range from musical
instruments to furniture. Here are some stories
about new uses for edible¹ materials.

¹ *edible:* safe to eat

1

To most people, carrots and other vegetables
are nothing more than salad ingredients. But
to a group of Austrian musicians, they are
also musical instruments. The members of the
Vegetable Orchestra got together in 1998 to explore
the musical possibilities of vegetables. They
create instruments by carving and cutting fresh
vegetables such as carrots, pumpkins, and radishes.
A carrot is a flute. A pumpkin becomes a drum.

2

Musicians from the Vienna Vegetable Orchestra play at a concert in Bordeaux, France.

A FACE OF FRUIT AND VEGETABLES

Arcimboldo (1527–1593) was an Italian painter who painted portraits of people. But his portraits were very unusual. He created them by painting a variety of objects such as fruits and vegetables. For example, in his work *Vertumnis*, Arcimboldo created a portrait of an emperor. In this painting, the emperor's nose is a small pear. His eyebrows are pea pods. He wears a crown of fruits and grains and his clothes are made of flowers and vegetables. People admired Arcimboldo's paintings during his lifetime, and his works are still popular today. You can see his paintings in The Louvre in Paris and in many other museums around the world.

Vertumnis

Radishes take the place of horns. The orchestra uses these vegetable instruments to play all kinds of contemporary and electronic music. Not surprisingly, the Vegetable Orchestra instruments are not like traditional instruments. Instead, they create totally original-sounding music.

Mothers often tell their children not to play with their food. But some artists don't listen. For example, Jim Victor creates large sculptures 3 of people, horses, and buildings from butter, cheese, and chocolate. There's a sculpture of a cow made entirely of butter, a replica of the Colosseum in Rome made from Parmesan cheese, and a life-sized chocolate car. Victor sculpts in a freezer to keep his materials from melting while he works. Another artist, photographer Balla Tamás, looks at food and sees humans and other creatures in everyday activities. He carves and then photographs creations made from fruits, vegetables, and other foods. For example, Tamás carved a man swimming in a pool from a watermelon. He used bananas to make a flying hummingbird and a dolphin coming out of the ocean.

Can you sit on a mushroom? Most people 4 would say no, but to one man, they make very good furniture. Phillip Ross is a mycologist. He studies fungi[2] such as mushrooms. Ross uses mushrooms to make building materials. His mushroom structures are as strong as concrete. He even makes his mushroom structures fire- and water-resistant.[3] This makes them excellent for use in buildings.

Food packaging, especially plastic, usually 5 ends up as garbage. It often causes environmental problems. David Edwards, a Harvard scientist, has a solution. He creates packaging from food. He creates plasticlike "skins" from fruits, vegetables, and other foods. The skins match the food they contain. For example, there is a tomato skin package for soup, an orange skin package for orange juice, and a chocolate skin package for chocolate milk. If you throw away the skin, it's safe for the environment. On the other hand, you could just simply eat it!

_____

[2] *fungi:* plantlike, nonflowering organisms that include mushrooms

[3] *fire- and water-resistant:* having qualities that make something almost impossible to be destroyed by fire and water

A food artist creates a sculpture out of cheddar cheese.

READING COMPREHENSION

Big Picture

A Work with a partner and choose the best heading for each of the following paragraphs.

1. Paragraph 2
   a. Original Instruments
   b. The Vegetable Orchestra
   c. Carrots, Pumpkins, and Radishes

2. Paragraph 3
   a. Food as Art
   b. Jim Victor and Balla Tamás
   c. Photographing Food

3. Paragraph 4
   a. Fire-Resistant Foods
   b. What a Mycologist Does
   c. Mushroom Furniture

B Compare answers to Exercise A with a partner. Then with your partner, write a heading for paragraph 5.

Close-Up

A Scan Reading 1 to find answers to the following questions. Write your answers on the lines.

1. What vegetables does the Vegetable Orchestra use to make the following instruments?

   a. _____ → horn

   b. _____ → flute

   c. _____ → drum

2. Where does Jim Victor usually work?

   In a _____ .

3. Why does Victor work there?

   To keep his _____ from _____ .

4. What did Victor use to make a sculpture of a car? _____

5. What did Balla Tamás use to make a sculpture of a man in a swimming pool? _____

6. What building material does the reading compare Phillip Ross's mushroom furniture to? _____

7. What food does David Edwards use to make the containers for the following items?

   a. _____ for chocolate milk

   b. _____ for orange juice

   c. _____ for tomato soup

8. What material does the reading compare Edwards's packaging to? _____

B Scan the short extra reading, "A Face of Fruit and Vegetables," on page 7 to answer the following questions.

1. When did Arcimboldo live?

2. Where are many of Arcimboldo's paintings?

3. What fruits and vegetables did Arcimboldo use in painting Vertumnis's face?

Reading Skill

Recognizing Word Forms

Some words have different forms for different parts of speech. For example, some words have noun and adjective forms. Nouns are people, places, and things. Adjectives describe nouns.

> Tamás carves and then photographs **creations** made from fruits, vegetables, and other foods.   noun

> Some very **creative** people are finding unexpected uses for food.
>   adjective

A The following statements are found in Reading 1. Write *N* if the word in bold in the sentence is a noun. Write *A* if the word in bold is an adjective.

_____ 1. The members of the Vegetable Orchestra got together in 1998 to explore the **musical** possibilities of vegetables. (Par. 2)

_____ 2. Not surprisingly, the Vegetable Orchestra instruments are not like **traditional** instruments. (Par. 2)

_____ 3. Instead, they create totally original-sounding **music**. (Par. 2)

_____ 4. It often causes **environmental** problems. (Par. 5)

_____ 5. If you throw the skin away, it's safe for the **environment**. (Par. 5)

B Use a dictionary to help you complete the chart below with the missing noun and adjective forms.

Noun	Adjective
art	
	creative
instrument	
	traditional

C Complete the following sentences with words from Exercises A and B.

1. a. Jim Victor has sculpted an unusual _____—a life-sized cow made from cheese.

   b. A very _____ architect built a hotel from ice.

2. a. My favorite kind of _____ is jazz.

   b. Lang Lang was a(n) _____ child. He learned to play the piano at the age of three.

3. a. The Vegetable Orchestra plays modern music. They don't play _____ music.

   b. Eating turkey is a holiday _____ in many parts of the world.

4. a. Victor taught _____ at the Pennsylvania Academy of the Fine Arts.

   b. A(n) _____ person often sees beauty in everyday objects.

5. a. Many people are concerned about the _____ problems that climate change causes.

   b. If you are concerned about the _____, you should recycle more and buy less.

6. a. The Vegetable Orchestra doesn't sing. Instead, they play _____ music.

   b. A(n) _____ made from a carrot sounds different from an instrument made from wood.

VOCABULARY PRACTICE

Academic Vocabulary

A Find the words in bold in Reading 1. Use the paragraph numbers to help you. Use the context to help you understand the meaning. Then match each word to the correct definition.

_b_ **1. instruments** (Par. 1)   **a.** things that are made or built

_e_ **2. materials** (Par. 1)   **b.** objects such as pianos or flutes that you play to make music

_d_ **3. explore** (Par. 2)   **c.** existing now

_c_ **4. contemporary** (Par. 2)   **d.** think about or discuss carefully; travel around a new place to find out what it's like

_a_ **5. structures** (Par. 4)   **e.** substances you need to make something

B The academic words in bold often appear with the words on the right. Find the words in bold in Reading 1. Circle the words that appear with them in the reading.

1. _____ **instruments**   musical / woodwind / stringed
2. **explore** _____   opportunities / ideas / possibilities
3. **contemporary** _____   art / music / architecture
4. _____ **materials**   building / strong / thick
5. _____ **structures**   safe / solid / fire-resistant

C Choose the best word on the right in Exercise B to go with an academic word on the left to complete the sentences below. Write the word combinations on the lines.

1. After art school, many students _____ in their field. They try to find jobs related to their studies.

2. People who play _____ often have better memories than people who don't.

3. Brick, wood, concrete, and steel are all common _____.

4. If you want to see _____, visit the Museum of Modern Art in New York City.

5. Houses that are built out of bricks are _____. They give a lot of protection, especially in places where there are a lot of high winds and strong rain.

Multiword Vocabulary

A Find the words in bold in Reading 1. Then write the words that come before and/or after them to complete the multiword vocabulary.

1. **range** ___from___ **musical instruments** _____ (Par. 1)
2. ___nothing___ **more** ___than___ (Par. 2)
3. ___to take___ **the place** ___of___ (Par. 2)
4. ___not___ **surprisingly** (Par. 2)
5. **ends** ___up___ **as** (Par. 5)
6. **throw** ___away___ (Par. 5)

B Complete the following sentences with the correct multiword vocabulary from Exercise A.

1. Glass is fire-resistant. _____, it makes a good building material.

2. Plastic often _____ garbage in the ocean. In fact, there's an island of plastic floating in the Pacific.

3. Food waste is a problem in wealthy countries. For example, studies show that Americans _____ 40 percent of the food they buy.

4. There's a surprising variety of instruments in the Vegetable Orchestra. They
_____ flutes _____ drums.

5. A carrot flute is a simple instrument. It's really _____ a
carrot with holes cut into it.

6. An edible skin, such as a tomato skin, can _____ plastic for
food packaging.

Use the Vocabulary

Write answers to the following questions. Use the words in bold in your answers. Then
share your answers with a partner.

1. Do you **throw away** a lot of food? What are some ways to avoid throwing away food?

2. What **materials** can **take the place of** plastic and also be good for the environment?

3. Do you like **contemporary art**? If not, what types of art do you prefer?

4. What subjects do you know very little about but would like to **explore**?

5. Are there any unusual or famous **structures** in your area? What are they? Why are they
unusual or famous?

6. What is your favorite **musical instrument**? Why is it your favorite?

THINK AND DISCUSS

Work in a small group. Use the information
in the reading and your own ideas to discuss
the following questions.

1. **Rank.** Of the four uses for food that you
read about in Reading 1, which one is the
most important or useful? Why?

2. **Express an opinion.** In your opinion, is
it wasteful to use food for art or musical
instruments? Explain your answer.

3. **Apply knowledge.** What is one use
for each of the following foods (other
than eating!)?

   pumpkins   chocolate
   mushrooms   bananas

Academic Vocabulary

energy	primary	a resource
a grant	a purpose	a vehicle

Multiword Vocabulary

along with	in some cases
to hold onto	to look into
in place of	a postage stamp

Reading Preview

A **Preview.** Skim Reading 2 by reading the first and last sentence of each paragraph. Then check (✓) four topics below that you think might be in this reading.

_____ 1. Different types of recipes that use coconut

_____ 2. Nonfood uses for coconuts

_____ 3. Using coconut as an energy source

_____ 4. Environmental uses of coconuts

_____ 5. Nutritional value of coconuts

_____ 6. Different uses for coconut husks

_____ 7. Climate needed for coconuts to grow

B **Topic vocabulary.** The following words appear in Reading 2. Look at the words and answer the questions with a partner.

amazing	lotion	petroleum
biofuel	multiple	renewable
containers	package	useful

1. Which words are adjectives? What do they mean?
2. Which words are liquids?
3. Which words are things that you can put other things inside?

C **Predict.** What do you think this reading will be about? Discuss each word in Exercise B and predict how it may relate to the reading.

Coconuts are nutritious and delicious. But those two facts aren't the main reasons why coconuts are so amazing. Coconuts have important uses, too—some old and some new.

Coconuts dry in the sun ready to be grated and shipped, Solomon Islands.

The Amazing Coconut

Y ou can put a postage stamp on it, you
can write an address on it, and you can
send it through the U.S. mail. No, it's
not an envelope or a package. It's the amazing
coconut! The coconut is different from most other
fruits because every part of it is useful. People
drink the milk and eat the meat. They use coconut oil as a lotion, and they use the husks¹ for

1

_____

¹ *husks:* the outside parts of some fruits, nuts, and seeds

coconuts for energy because coconuts are cheap, clean, and renewable. Already, coconut-rich countries such as Papua New Guinea, the Philippines, and Vanuatu[2] are using coconut oil for this purpose. Engineers from these countries have made an effective biofuel out of coconut oil and alcohol. The fuel can power cars, trucks, ships, and even electric-power plants. In addition, the South Pacific islands of Tokelau[3] are using coconut oil along with solar energy as their primary energy source. The two together can produce 100 percent of the electricity the islands need.

3　Students at Baylor University in Texas received a grant to study the coconut husk. One useful feature of the fibers of the husk is that they can take in water very well. Mixing coconut husks with dry soil helps the soil to hold onto more of the water. The students are also finding that the fibers can replace plastic in some cases. For example, the students are looking into using coconut husk fibers instead of plastic in parts of car interiors. If this is possible, it will help to make vehicles more environmentally friendly.

4　The husk of the coconut is a perfect package. It protects the coconut from damage. When the coconut falls on the ground or into water, the husk protects it. Its strong husk is the reason the U.S. Postal Service allows people to send the coconut without any extra packaging anywhere in the country. All that is necessary is to stick some stamps right onto the coconut. Each year, tourists on the Hawaiian island of Molokai post about 3,000 of these "coconut postcards."

5　Coconuts grow naturally in over 80 countries of the world. They require only sun and regular rainfall. No extra care is needed. Every year, these 80 countries produce more than 61 million tons of coconuts. It is not surprising, then, that people want to find multiple uses for the coconut. Because they're an easy-to-grow resource, coconuts really are more than just great souvenirs to bring home after a trip to the tropics.

containers. People in some island nations have even used the coconut in place of money. It is possible that humans have been using coconuts in many of these different ways for thousands of years. Even today, people are still finding new uses for the coconut.

2　One of the more exciting uses of the coconut is as a source of energy in place of petroleum. Scientists around the world are working on using

---

[2] *Papua New Guinea, the Philippines, and Vanuatu:* island nations or independent states in the South Pacific

[3] *Tokelau:* a territory of New Zealand that consists of three islands

READING COMPREHENSION

Big Picture

A The following statements are the main ideas of some of the paragraphs in Reading 2. Write the correct paragraph number next to its main idea.

_____ **1.** The coconut husk protects the coconut.

_____ **2.** The coconut can be used as an alternative energy source.

_____ **3.** The coconut has many different uses.

_____ **4.** Students are exploring different uses for the coconut husk.

B Every author has a purpose for writing a text. Read the list below. Check (✓) the author's purpose for writing Reading 2.

_____ **1.** To persuade people to grow more coconuts

_____ **2.** To show how valuable and useful the coconut is

_____ **3.** To give people ideas for alternative sources of energy

Close-Up

A Complete the chart below by listing all the past and current uses of the parts of the coconut mentioned in Reading 2.

	Uses
coconut oil	
coconut milk and meat	
coconut husks	
the whole coconut	

B Compare answers to Exercise A with a partner. For each part of the coconut, choose what you think is its most important use and least important use. Give reasons for your choices.

Reading Skill

A Read the following questions. Focus on the key words in **bold**. Then quickly scan the paragraph below for the answers. Write short answers.

1. What are **electrolytes**? _____

2. When do people **lose electrolytes**? _____

3. **What kind** of **coconut** has a lot of electrolytes? _____

4. What other problems in addition to **dehydration** does loss of electrolytes cause?

   _____

5. What works **in the same way** as green coconut water? _____

   Most people are familiar with the use of coconut oil in hair shampoo, but less well-known are some of the medical uses of coconuts. For example, the water from a young, or green, coconut is full of electrolytes, minerals in your blood that carry an electric charge. When athletes train, or anyone exercises hard, they sweat. When they sweat, they lose electrolytes. This can lead to dehydration, nausea, and even vomiting. Green coconut water is full of electrolytes. It is a natural solution for these problems. The electrolytes in the coconut water give people energy. Therefore, coconut water works in the same way as popular energy drinks.

B Read the following questions about Reading 2. Underline the key word(s) in each question. Then quickly scan the reading to find the answers. Write short answers.

1. How many years have people been using the coconut? _____

2. What feature of the husk makes it so useful to mix with soil? _____

3. Where is the coconut being used with solar energy? _____

4. Baylor University students are looking into using coconut husks for which part of the car?

   _____

5. In how many countries do coconuts grow naturally? _____

VOCABULARY PRACTICE

Academic Vocabulary

A Find the words in bold in Reading 2. Use the paragraph numbers to help you. Use the context to help you understand the meaning. Then match each word to the definition.

_d_ **1. energy** (Par. 2)　　　　**a.** the thing you want to achieve

_a_ **2. purpose** (Par. 2)　　　　**b.** the most important or most depended on

_b_ **3. primary** (Par. 2)　　　　**c.** something a country has and can use to increase its wealth

_e_ **4. grant** (Par. 3)　　　　**d.** the power that makes machines work

_f_ **5. vehicles** (Par. 3)　　　　**e.** money given to people to do something specific

_c_ **6. resource** (Par. 5)　　　　**f.** machines that carry people or things

B Read the following sentences and choose the best word or phrase to complete each one. The correct word often appears with the word in bold. Write the word on the line.

1. The use of _____b_____ **energy** in the future will help solve many environmental problems.

   a. unnatural　　　　**b.** renewable　　　　**c.** white

2. A team of researchers went to the South Pacific _____ **purpose** of studying wave energy.

   a. for the　　　　**b.** out of the　　　　**c.** according to the

3. Their **primary** _____ for changing from petroleum to solar power is that solar power is renewable and cheap.

   a. tool　　　　**b.** need　　　　**c.** reason

4. Many scientists and university professors _____ **grants** from the government or private industry to do their research.

   a. make　　　　**b.** serve　　　　**c.** receive

5. _____ **vehicles**—that is, vehicles with more than one passenger—can travel in the car-pool lane.

   a. Human　　　　**b.** High-occupancy　　　　**c.** Travel

6. Sunshine is a(n) _____ **resource**. There's always more, so that's why solar energy is a good solution to our energy problems.

   a. renewable　　　　**b.** money　　　　**c.** original

Multiword Vocabulary

A Find the words in bold in Reading 2. Then write the words that come before and/or after them to complete the multiword vocabulary.

1. _____post_____ **stamp** (Par. 1)　　　　4. **hold** _____onto_____ (Par. 3)

2. **in place** _____of_____ (Par. 1)　　　　5. **in some** _____cas_____ (Par. 3)

3. **along** _____with_____ (Par. 2)　　　　6. **looking** _____into_____ (Par. 3)

B Complete the following sentences with the correct multiword vocabulary from Exercise A. Use the words in parentheses to help you.

1. The price of a(n) _____ (a small piece of paper that shows you have paid to mail something) goes up all the time.

2. Students usually need four years to graduate, but _____ (sometimes) they can finish faster.

3. Hybrid cars use battery power _____ (in addition to) gasoline to power the car's engine.

4. The fastest solution is not always the best solution. Taking your time and _____ (exploring) all the possibilities is sometimes better than acting quickly.

5. People with certain illnesses are unable to _____ (keep) the nutrition they get from the food they eat.

6. Schools are trying to get children to eat nutritious snacks such as fruit and vegetables _____ (instead of) fattening foods such as cookies and chips.

Use the Vocabulary

Write answers to the following questions. Use the words in bold in your answers. Then share your answers with a partner.

1. Think of a country that you know well. What natural **resources** does it have and how are they used?

2. Do you know any people who **hold onto** old-fashioned or traditional ideas? Give examples of the ideas they are **holding onto**.

3. How many different career paths or college programs is it important to **look into** before choosing one?

4. If you needed to eat healthier food, what changes could you make in your life? What things could you eat **in place of** some of the things you usually eat now?

5. If you received a **grant** to study something, what would you study?

6. What do you think the future of the **postage stamp** will be now that most people communicate less and less by regular mail?

7. What do you think is the **primary purpose** of taking tests in English classes?

THINK AND DISCUSS

Work in a small group. Use the information in the reading and your own ideas to discuss the following questions.

1. **Apply knowledge.** What kinds of companies would be interested in giving students grant money to study coconut husks? Give reasons for your answers.

2. **Synthesize.** Why do you think small island nations in the South Pacific are among the first nations to become independent of petroleum? Are these island nations good models for other countries? Why, or why not?

3. **Analyze.** Why do you think some islanders used coconuts in place of money? What things do we use in place of money now?

Vocabulary Review

(A) Complete the paragraphs with the vocabulary below that you have studied in the unit.

along with	in place of	renewable energy
exploring the possibility	not surprisingly	threw away
for the purpose of	primary source	

Many things that we eat can have other important uses. For example, some foods are used as fuel, ink, or medicine.

Corn. Corn can be made into ethanol. It can be used instead of gasoline in cars. _____ , many people think that using corn instead of gasoline is a good thing.

         1
Corn is a _____ source that can last forever and help keep our planet clean.

         2

Soybeans. Soy is a _____ of food for many people in many parts of the

         3
world. Soybeans can be used _____ making environmentally friendly ink. In

         4
the past, inks used for printing contained petroleum. This made ink expensive and dangerous for the environment when people _____ printed paper. Using soy

         5
_____ petroleum is healthier for the environment and for the people who

         6
work with ink.

Chili Peppers. _____ adding flavor and nutrition to cuisines all over the

         7
world, peppers also play an important role in medicine. Capsaicin, a chemical in peppers, can help people who have pain on their skin, in their muscles, or in their joints. Researchers are also
_____ of using capsaicin in weight reduction.

         8

B Compare answers to Exercise A with a partner. Then discuss the following question.

Which use of food in Exercise A seems the most important? Why?

C Complete the following sentences in a way that shows that you understand the meaning of the words in bold.

1. You can avoid having things **end up as** garbage if you _____ .

2. In my life, nothing can **take the place of** _____ .

3. An example of a **resource** that is not **renewable** is _____ .

4. One advantage of having a **high-occupancy vehicle** is _____ .

D Work with a partner and write four sentences that include any four of the vocabulary items below. You may use any verb tense and make nouns plural if you want.

a fire-resistant structure	look into	range from . . . to
hold onto	a musical instrument	receive a grant

Connect the Readings

A Look back at Readings 1 and 2 to complete the chart below. Put a check (✓) in the boxes to show which topics appeared in each reading. Note that some topics appeared in both readings.

	Reading 1	Reading 2
1. Fun uses for foods		
2. Artistic uses for foods		
3. Practical uses for foods		
4. Environmental uses for foods		

B With a partner or in a small group, compare answers to Exercise A. Then discuss the following questions.

1. What are some examples from the readings of each of the topics in Exercise A?

2. What are some examples of fun, artistic, practical, and environmental uses for foods that are not mentioned in the readings?

C Discuss the following questions with a partner. Use your understanding of the readings and your own ideas.

1. Which ten foods do you think it would be most difficult for humans to live without? Explain your answer.

2. What is another food that has many different uses?

3. What are some other natural, non-food materials that have many different uses?

The Face

FOCUS

1. Which do you remember more easily: new names or new faces?

2. When you describe someone to another person, what parts of the person's face do you usually talk about?

A Balinese dancer in costume and makeup in Bali, Indonesia

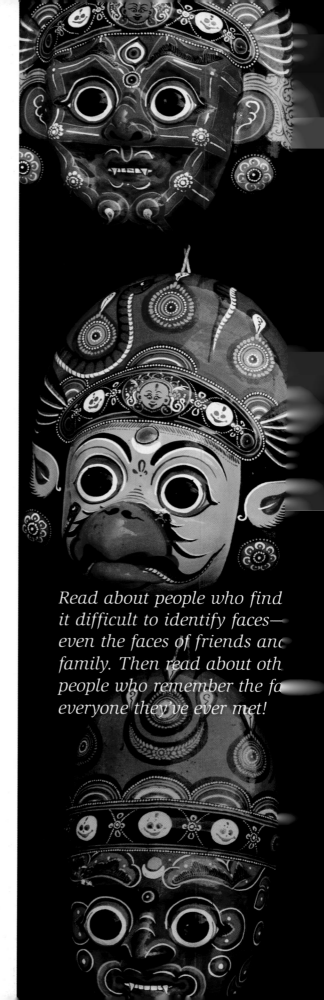

Academic Vocabulary

aware	considerably	skilled
to compensate	a section	a technique

Multiword Vocabulary

to be responsible for	it turns out that
for the time being	on the other hand
in the process of	to some degree

Reading Preview

A **Preview.** Skim through Reading 1 on pages 28–29 by reading the first and last sentences of each paragraph. Then discuss the following questions with a partner or in a small group.

1. Do you ever have problems recognizing someone you have met before? How does it make you feel?

2. Do you know people who look alike? In what ways do they look alike?

3. Imagine you have trouble recognizing faces. What problems might that cause?

B **Topic vocabulary.** The following words appear in Reading 1. Look at the words and answer the questions with a partner.

blindness	condition	mirror
brain	cure	recognition
colorblind	forget	remember

1. Which words are most closely related to sight?

2. Which words are most closely related to memory?

3. Which words can be used to discuss health problems?

C **Predict.** What do you think this reading will be about? Discuss each word in Exercise B and predict how it may relate to the reading.

Read about people who find it difficult to identify faces—even the faces of friends and family. Then read about oth[er] people who remember the fa[ce of] everyone they've ever met!

Face Blindness

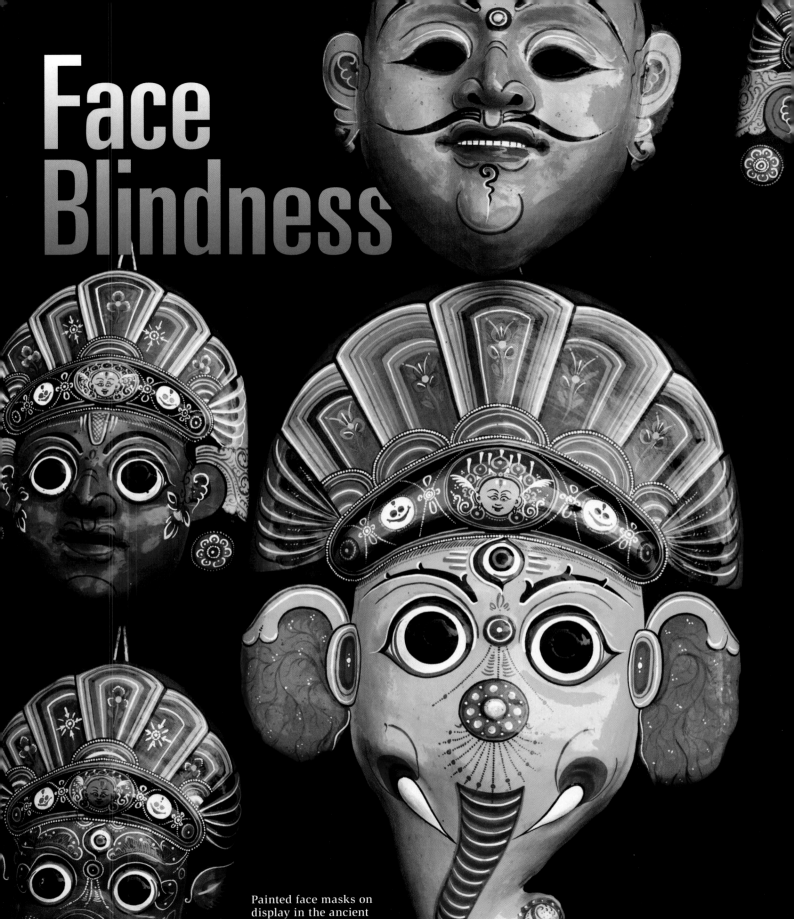

Painted face masks on display in the ancient city of Bhaktapur, Nepal

The first thing we notice about new people are their faces. The next time we see these people, we remember them because we remember their faces. This seems like a simple process. It turns out, however, that when scientists looked into the brain, they found that face recognition is not such a simple process. The section of the brain that is responsible for face recognition seems to work differently for different people. Some people have great difficulty remembering and recognizing faces, while others almost never forget a face.

Normal babies are born with a natural ability to recognize faces. In fact, their face-recognition abilities are much better than their parents. For example, most adults can easily recognize faces that are similar to their own. However, they cannot easily recognize faces of people of different races. Babies can. They can even recognize faces of different animals such as monkeys. At six months, babies are highly skilled at face recognition. But by nine months, they lose this skill. By nine months, a baby's face-recognition skills are about the same as an adult's.

Unfortunately, some people are not born with this ability to recognize faces. The part of the brain that is responsible for face recognition doesn't work for them. This condition is called *prosopagnosia*, or "face blindness." People with very severe face blindness cannot even recognize their own faces. In fact, people with this condition can sometimes be frightened when they look in the mirror. They don't recognize their own face, so for a second they are startled[1] when they see this unfamiliar face.

Face blindness is not always severe. Some people only have difficulty recognizing faces of people they don't know very well. Scientists believe up to 10 percent of the population may

---

[1] *startled:* slightly surprised or frightened by something you did not expect

be affected by face blindness to some degree, yet many people with mild face blindness might not even know they have it. They have no reason to know that they are different from anyone else until someone points it out. This is similar to people with color blindness. Colorblind people can't see the difference between certain colors such as red and green. Until someone tells them that green and red are two different colors, they don't know that other people see those colors differently.

Scientists became aware of another face-recognition condition in the process of researching face blindness. They found that there are also "super recognizers." Super recognizers remember every face they have ever seen. For these people, it is not possible to forget faces. Super recognizer Jennifer Jarrett says, "It's as if they [faces] are cemented[2]

"Some people have great difficulty remembering and recognizing faces, while others almost never forget a face."

5

_____

[2] *cemented:* fixed; glued; stuck

in my brain." Many super recognizers don't just recognize faces they have seen before. They know exactly where they last saw that person. Jarrett has many stories of this happening. One time she recognized a person she had only seen once many years earlier. This person had been her waitress at a restaurant. This person had aged and changed considerably. Still, Jarrett knew exactly where she had seen her last.

Super recognizers don't usually feel that they have a problem. Most people with moderate to severe face blindness, on the other hand, do. There is no cure for face blindness. So for the time being, people with face blindness need to find simple techniques to compensate for their problem. They can try to recognize people by their hairstyle, their voice, or their glasses. Hopefully, in the future as scientists learn more about this condition, they will find a cure.

6

READING COMPREHENSION

Big Picture

Ⓐ Choose the answer that best completes each of the following sentences.

1. The reading discusses _____ unusual types of face-recognition conditions in adults.
   a. two   b. three   c. four   d. five

2. According to the reading, most people _____.
   a. learn face-recognition skills   b. are born with face-recognition skills

3. "Super recognizers" have a condition that is _____ the condition of face blindness.
   a. similar to   b. the opposite of

Ⓑ Compare answers to Exercise A with a partner. Point out the places in the reading that show that your answers are correct.

Close-Up

Ⓐ Decide which of the following statements are true or false according to the reading. Write *T* (True) or *F* (False) next to each one.

_____ 1. Scientists are still looking for the part of the brain humans use to recognize faces.

_____ 2. A baby who is six months old can recognize faces better than an adult can.

_____ 3. Humans' face-recognition skills improve as they get older.

_____ 4. Most people can recognize different monkeys of the same type by their faces.

_____ 5. Some people with severe prosopagnosia cannot recognize themselves in the mirror.

_____ 6. People with mild prosopagnosia don't always know that they have it.

_____ 7. "Super recognizers" use strategies and techniques to memorize faces.

_____ 8. Scientists are working on ways to help people with prosopagnosia.

Ⓑ Work with a partner or in a small group. Change the false statements in Exercise A to make them true.

Reading Skill

Identifying Main Ideas

Every reading has one main idea, and each paragraph has one main idea that supports it. Good readers look for the main idea of the whole reading. They also look for the main idea of each paragraph. While they are reading, they ask themselves, "What is the main idea of this paragraph?" and "How does this main idea support the main idea of the whole reading?"

A Read the following statements. Check (✓) the statement that expresses the main idea of the *whole* reading.

_____ **1.** The ability to recognize faces is not the same for everyone.

_____ **2.** Being able to recognize faces is an important social skill.

_____ **3.** Everyone can learn to be a "super recognizer" of faces.

B The following statements are the main ideas of paragraphs 2–5 in Reading 1. Write the correct paragraph number next to its main idea.

_____ **1.** There are different levels of face blindness.

_____ **2.** Babies' face-recognition skills change as they develop.

_____ **3.** Some people have a condition that is almost the opposite of prosopagnosia.

_____ **4.** Some people have a condition called *prosopagnosia*.

VOCABULARY PRACTICE

Academic Vocabulary

A Find the words in bold in Reading 1. Use the context to help you match each word to the correct definition.

_b_ **1. section** (Par. 1)   **a.** having good ability

_a_ **2. skilled** (Par. 2)   **b.** part

_d_ **3. aware** (Par. 5)   **c.** do something to make a situation better

_f_ **4. considerably** (Par. 5)   **d.** knowing something

_e_ **5. techniques** (Par. 6)   **e.** strategies; methods

_c_ **6. compensate** (Par. 6)   **f.** very much

B Read the following sentences and choose the best word to complete each one.

1. The managers aren't yet **aware** _____ the problem.
   a. of   **b.** to   **c.** for

2. According to scientists, at least one **section** _____ the brain is responsible for face recognition.
   a. for   **b.** into   **c.** of

3. Jared has difficulty remembering his students' names. He **compensates** _____ this by making notes about each student's appearance on the attendance sheet.
   a. for   **b.** to   **c.** of

4. After completing the language course, the students were **considerably** _____ at understanding English.
   a. good   **b.** better   **c.** best

5. The employment agency is looking for people who are highly **skilled** _____ fixing computers.
   a. at   **b.** for   **c.** with

6. A _____ **technique** that some people with face blindness use is to act as if they know everyone.
   a. fast   **b.** severe   **c.** simple

Multiword Vocabulary

A Find the multiword vocabulary in bold in Reading 1. Use the context to help you understand the meaning. Then match each item to the correct definition.

_d_ **1. it turns out** (Par. 1)   **a.** looking at it in another way

_b_ **2. is responsible for** (Par. 1)   **b.** takes care of

_e_ **3. to some degree** (Par. 4)   **c.** until something changes

_f_ **4. in the process of** (Par. 5)   **d.** it became clear that

_a_ **5. on the other hand** (Par. 6)   **e.** to a certain extent

_c_ **6. for the time being** (Par. 6)   **f.** while

B Complete the following paragraph with the correct multiword vocabulary from Exercise A.

   I have always had problems recognizing people. I recently discovered, though, that I shouldn't be ashamed of this because _____ I have a condition called
_____1_____
prosopagnosia. I don't have a severe case, but I do have it _____.
                                                                              _____2_____
Now I'm working with an occupational therapist. She _____
                                                                          _____3_____
helping me develop strategies to deal with the condition. I live in a small town, so
_____ going shopping, I often see people who recognize me. I'm
_____4_____
sure it bothers them when I don't recognize them. This morning, I was out shopping. It was 11:30, and I was feeling good because I hadn't run into anyone. Then, suddenly, an unfamiliar face approached me. I felt that I was supposed to know the person. I started to feel nervous as I wondered who the person was. Perhaps I should wear a sign that says, "I have face blindness."
_____ , perhaps _____ , I
_____5_____   _____6_____
should just stay at home!

Use the Vocabulary

Write answers to the following questions. Use the words in bold in your answers. Then share your answers with a partner.

1. Are you **in the process of** making any changes in your home, work, or school situation? In your life in general? If so, what are you **in the process of** changing?

2. What **techniques** do you use to memorize new words?

3. What is something you think you are particularly **skilled at**? When did you first become **aware of** having that ability?

4. When you are trying to explain something in English, but you don't know the vocabulary words that you need, how do you **compensate**?

THINK AND DISCUSS

Work in a small group. Use the information in the reading and your own ideas to discuss the following questions.

1. **Relate to personal experience.** How good are your face-recognition skills? Give reasons for your answer.

2. **Make connections.** According to the reading, 10 percent of people could have some degree of face blindness. Do you know anyone who you think might have this problem? What makes you think that?

3. **Analyze.** What do you think might be the advantages and disadvantages of being a "super recognizer"?

4. **Apply knowledge.** Imagine you are a teacher with a severe form of face blindness. What could you do to compensate?

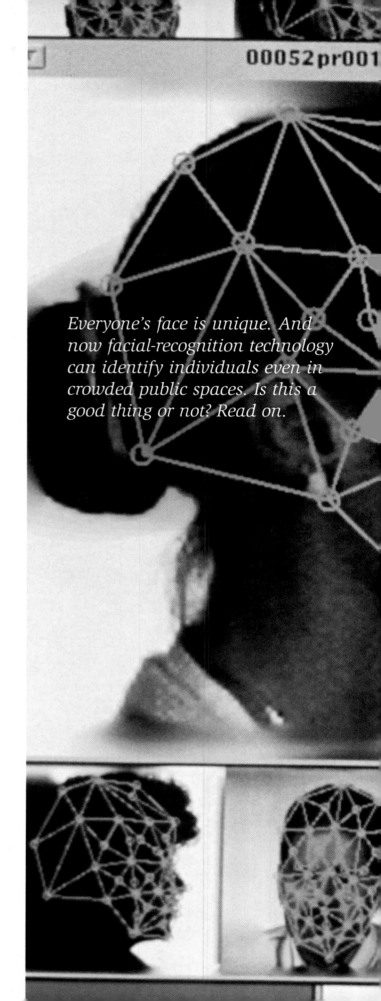

00052pr001

Academic Vocabulary

to analyze	a benefit	a feature
an area	a code	unique

Multiword Vocabulary

to be concerned about	an invasion of privacy
identity theft	social media
in the meantime	to take a picture

Reading Preview

Ⓐ Preview. Skim Reading 2 by reading the first and last sentence of each paragraph. Then check (✓) four topics below that you think might be in this reading.

_____ **1.** Reasons why facial-recognition technology is illegal in most countries

_____ **2.** How banks might make use of facial recognition technology in the future

_____ **3.** Physical characteristics that make people beautiful

_____ **4.** People's concerns about the use of facial-recognition technology

_____ **5.** Potential uses of facial-recognition technology in marketing

_____ **6.** Companies who sell pictures of other people without their permission

_____ **7.** Information that might be stored by using facial-recognition technology

Ⓑ Topic vocabulary. The following words appear in Reading 2. Look at the words and answer the questions with a partner.

cheeks	facial	software
database	nose	space
distances	points	Web site

1. Which words relate to technology?

2. Which words relate to faces?

3. Which words relate to measurement?

Ⓒ Predict. What do you think this reading will be about? Discuss each word in Exercise B and predict how it may relate to the reading.

Everyone's face is unique. And now facial-recognition technology can identify individuals even in crowded public spaces. Is this a good thing or not? Read on.

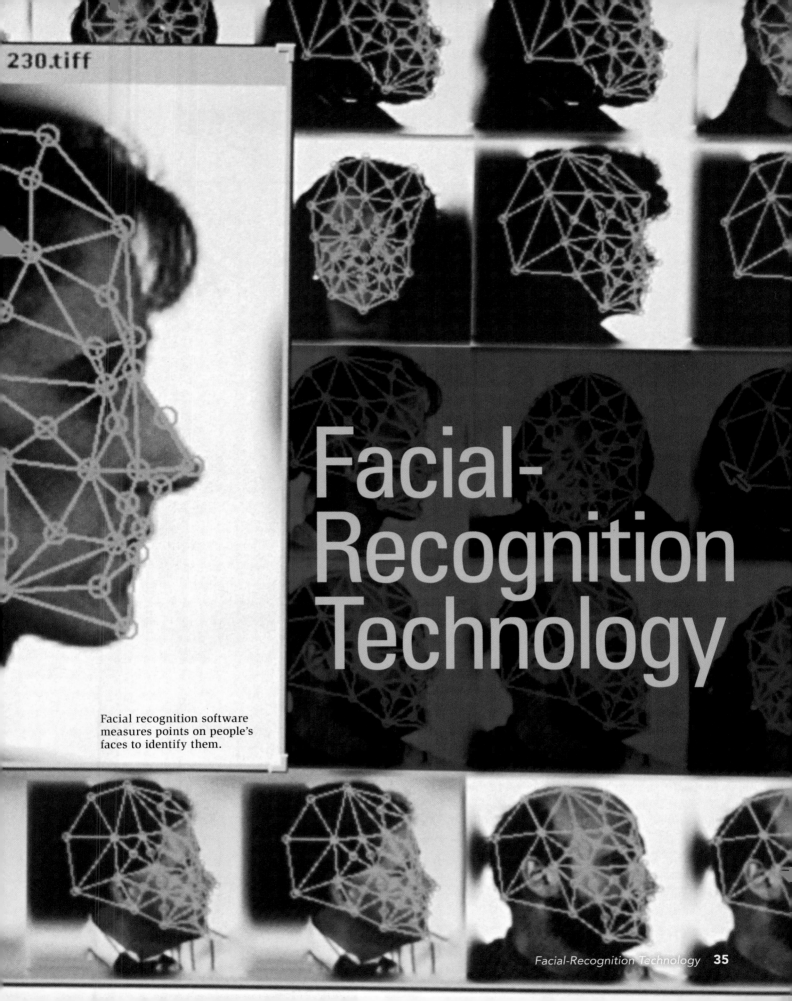

230.tiff

Facial-Recognition Technology

Facial recognition software measures points on people's faces to identify them.

IDENTITY PROTECTION

Name:
Password:

F aces communicate feelings. They can 1 tell people if we are happy, sad, or confused. Faces have another use, too. Your face can identify you. It is unique, like a fingerprint. Unless you have an identical twin, there is no one else in the world with your face. Now, organizations are using your face for many different purposes. This could be very helpful, but some people have concerns about using faces for identification.

Today, computer software can recognize 2 faces. Just like fingers, faces have unique features that we can measure. For example, every face has high points and low points. There are high points such as your cheeks or your nose and low points such as the space between your nose and your cheek. Facial-recognition technology measures the distances between these points. The software saves these measurements in a database as a code. Each code represents a particular face. The software can take the code of any new face—for example, a person in a crowd—and match it to the codes for faces that are already in the database. If the codes match, it's probably the same person.

One use of facial-recognition technology is in police work. Police departments use facial-recognition databases to identify people just like they use collections of fingerprints. For example, police used this technology after September 11, 2001, at a large sports event in Tampa Bay, Florida, to look for terrorists. In this case, the police analyzed the data from the facial-recognition technology and found that there were no terrorists at the game. Another use is for preventing identity theft. One company is developing software for banks. Banks will use a customer's "faceprint" for identification instead of a PIN[1] or ID card, which are easy to steal. This way, it will be difficult for identity thieves to pretend that they are bank customers.

"Just like fingers, faces have unique features that we can measure."

Not everyone is happy with these developments. Many people feel that facial-recognition technology can be an invasion of privacy. For example, advertisers are using the technology to analyze people's faces. When people walk by an outdoor ad—for example, in a shopping area—the sign takes their picture. It analyzes the picture and then suggests products for these people to buy, such as makeup. People have another concern: A stranger may take your picture without your knowledge. This person can then use the technology to match this photo of you to one on a social media Web site. These sites often have personal information about you such as your age, your interests, and even your address. Naturally, people are concerned about this. No one wants a stranger who takes their photo in a public place to find out detailed facts about them.

Does facial-recognition technology provide important benefits or problems? Experts hope that we will find ways to limit the risks of the technology. It's possible that as the new technology develops, we will need new laws to protect people. In the meantime, experts have a suggestion: Simply tilt[2] your head 15 degrees to the side when someone takes your picture. Facial recognition doesn't work on faces in this position!

---

[1] *PIN:* personal identification number; a secret number that people use with a bankcard to withdraw money

[2] *tilt:* move slightly up, down, or to one side

READING COMPREHENSION

Big Picture

A Read the following list of ideas. Check (✓) the five ideas that express the main ideas of Reading 2.

_✓_ **1.** How facial-recognition software works

_____ **2.** How the brain recognizes faces

_✓_ **3.** Laws about when the police can use facial-recognition technology

_✓_ **4.** Some uses of a technology that recognizes faces

_✓_ **5.** How we can use faces to identify people

_✓_ **6.** Good uses and bad uses of software that recognizes faces

_✓_ **7.** How facial-recognition software invades our privacy

_____ **8.** Tips for recognizing people

B Compare answers to Exercise A with a partner. Then discuss what you think the main idea of the whole reading is.

Close-Up

(A) Choose the answer that best completes each of the following sentences, according to the reading.

1. The police used the technology to look for _____ at an event in Florida.
   a. identity thieves
   b. terrorists

2. Banks can use the technology to _____.
   a. prevent identity theft
   b. increase profits

3. Companies can use images of people's faces to _____.
   a. create ads
   b. improve products

4. People can match a photo to an online photo and _____.
   a. sell you things
   b. get personal information about you

(B) Compare answers to Exercise A with a partner. Discuss which sentences show something positive about facial-recognition technology and which show something negative.

Reading Skill

Recognizing Supporting Information

Supporting information tells you more about the main idea of a paragraph. Supporting information can be details, facts, and examples that explain or give a clear picture of the main idea. They often answer the reader's questions about main ideas such as *Who*, *What*, *How*, *When*, *Where*, and *Why*.

(A) Read the following paragraph and underline the main idea.

It is possible that GPS in smartphones presents a new way to invade our privacy. GPS means "global positioning system." Most smartphones come with GPS. GPS in phones shows where the phone is. This means, of course, that it also shows where the person *with* the phone is. GPS makes it possible to follow people as they move from place to place and to always know exactly where they are. If someone knows where you are, they can often guess information such as what you're doing and who you are doing it with. Many people feel that software that can show where you are at any time is a threat to privacy.

(B) Use the supporting information in Exercise A to answer the following questions. Write short answers.

1. **What** does "GPS" mean?

   _____

2. **Where** do you often find GPS?

   _____

3. What does GPS in phones show?

_____

4. What information can a person guess by watching where you go?

_____

5. Why are some people unhappy with GPS?

_____

C Reread paragraph 2 in Reading 2 and underline the main idea. Then answer the following questions. Write short answers.

1. How are faces and fingerprints similar?

unique features

2. What high points and low points on the face can we measure?

cHeeks

3. What does facial-recognition technology measure on the face?

Database

4. How is information about faces saved?

_____

5. What does it mean when a code for a face in a crowd matches a code for a face in a database?

_____

VOCABULARY PRACTICE

Academic Vocabulary

A Find the words in the box below in Reading 2. Use the context and the words in parentheses to help you choose the correct word to complete each of the following sentences.

unique (Par. 1)	code (Par. 2)	area (Par. 4)
features (Par. 2)	analyzed (Par. 3)	benefits (Par. 5)

1. Some actors use surgery to change their _features_ (the parts of a face such as the eyes or the nose) in order to look younger.

2. Everyone's fingerprints are _unique_ (one of a kind). In other words, no one has exactly the same fingerprints.

3. It's not a good idea to drive at night in a(n) _Area_ (place) that has a lot of crime.

4. What are the _benefits_ (positive things) of smartphones that make them so useful?

5. Identity thieves often need to know your zip _code_ (a set of numbers that represent some information) in order to use your credit card.

6. The police _____ (looked at carefully) the handwriting, but could not decide who had written the note.

B The academic words in bold often appear with the words on the right. Find the words in bold in Reading 2. Circle the words that appear with them in the reading.

1. **unique** _____   ideas / personality / features

2. _____ **area**   shopping / remote / urban

3. _____ **benefits**   unexpected / important / main

4. **analyzed** _____   the situation / the data / the content

C Choose the best word on the right in Exercise B to go with an academic word on the left to complete the sentences below. Write the word combinations on the lines.

1. Cell phones won't usually work in a(n) _Remote Area_ such as in a forest or on a mountaintop.

2. The police often ask witnesses to describe the _unique features_ of someone's face such as a large nose or a beard.

3. After the research scientists had _Analyzed the data_ from the experiment, they decided to publish the results in a science journal.

4. Many cell phone customers were surprised when they found their phones had speech-recognition software and a high-definition camera. Those were certainly _unexpected benefits._

Multiword Vocabulary

A Find the words in bold in Reading 2. Then write the words that come before and/or after them to complete the multiword vocabulary.

1. **identity** _theft_ (Par. 3)

2. **an invasion of** _Privacy_ (Par. 4)

3. **social** _media_ (Par. 4)

4. **are concerned** _about_ (Par. 4)

5. _In the_ **meantime** (Par. 5)

6. **takes your** _Picture_ (Par. 5)

B Complete the following sentences with the correct multiword vocabulary from Exercise A.

1. People communicate with their friends on _Social media_ Web sites such as Facebook.

2. Is it illegal if someone _Take_ without asking first?

3. If you _are concerned_ something, you are worried about it.

4. _Identity theft_ _an invasion of Privacy_ is when someone uses your personal information to steal from you.

5. I'm saving money to buy a professional camera someday. _In the meantime_, I'll use the camera on my phone.

6. A GPS can be _____ because it tells people where you are.

Use the Vocabulary

Write answers to the following questions. Use the words in bold in your answers. Then share your answers with a partner.

1. Describe the facial **features** of a friend or a family member. What makes this person's face **unique**?

2. What are the **main benefits** of your cell phone?

3. Do you ever **analyze** books or movies after you read or see them? If so, what are some examples of books or movies that you have **analyzed**? Explain your answers.

4. Which kinds of technology do you think are **an invasion of** people's **privacy**? **Are** you **concerned about** privacy issues? Why, or why not?

5. Which **social media** sites do you use the most? Why do you like these sites?

6. Do you like to **take pictures**? If yes, what do you **take pictures** of?

THINK AND DISCUSS

Work in a small group. Use the information in the reading and your own ideas to discuss the following questions.

1. **Analyze.** Do you think it is acceptable for companies to use facial-recognition software in order to sell products to you? Why, or why not?

2. **Relate to personal experience.** Are there pictures of you on the Internet? Do you worry that someone might be able to use your photo to steal your identity?

3. **Express an opinion.** What is your opinion of facial-recognition technology? Do you think it provides more benefits or more problems?

Vocabulary Review

A Complete the paragraphs with the vocabulary below that you have studied in the unit.

compensates for 2	takes a picture of 6
important benefit 8	to some degree 4
it turns out 1	unique features 5
a simple technique 3	was concerned about 7

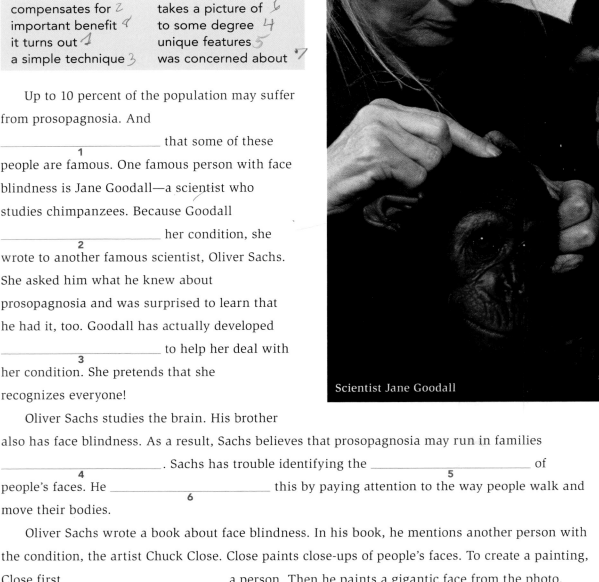

Scientist Jane Goodall

Up to 10 percent of the population may suffer from prosopagnosia. And _____ that some of these
1
people are famous. One famous person with face blindness is Jane Goodall—a scientist who studies chimpanzees. Because Goodall _____ her condition, she
2
wrote to another famous scientist, Oliver Sachs. She asked him what he knew about prosopagnosia and was surprised to learn that he had it, too. Goodall has actually developed _____ to help her deal with
3
her condition. She pretends that she recognizes everyone!

Oliver Sachs studies the brain. His brother also has face blindness. As a result, Sachs believes that prosopagnosia may run in families _____. Sachs has trouble identifying the _____ of
4   **5**
people's faces. He _____ this by paying attention to the way people walk and
6
move their bodies.

Oliver Sachs wrote a book about face blindness. In his book, he mentions another person with the condition, the artist Chuck Close. Close paints close-ups of people's faces. To create a painting, Close first _____ a person. Then he paints a gigantic face from the photo.
7
Close sells those paintings for thousands of dollars. But they have another _____: Close says the process helps him to better remember people's faces.
8

B Compare answers to Exercise A with a partner. Then discuss the following question.

Which technique for remembering faces—Goodall's, Sachs's, or Close's—do you think is the most effective and why?

C Complete the following sentences in a way that shows that you understand the meaning of the words in bold.

1. I don't want to move to **a remote area** because _____.

2. **An invasion of privacy** to me is _____.

3. **In the process of** becoming an adult, _____.

4. People can **age considerably** when _____.

D Work with a partner and write four sentences that include any four of the vocabulary items below. You may use any verb tense and make nouns plural if you want.

analyze data	on the other hand	a section of
for the time being	responsible for	social media

Connect the Readings

A Look back at Readings 1 and 2 to answer the questions in the chart below. Write notes in the boxes.

	Reading 1	Reading 2
1. What aspect of facial recognition does each reading focus on?		
2. What problem connected with facial recognition does each reading present?		
3. What solutions do the readings suggest in their conclusions?		

B With a partner or in a small group, compare answers to Exercise A. Then discuss the following questions.

1. In what ways are the abilities of super recognizers similar to the functions of facial-recognition technology?

2. Compare the problems and solutions suggested in the conclusions. Which problem do you think will have a solution sooner? Give reasons for your choice.

C Discuss the following questions with a partner. Use your understanding of the readings and your own ideas.

1. What would be a good job for a super recognizer?

2. If you could invent one application of facial-recognition technology that would make your life more convenient, what would it be?

3. People and computers don't only use faces to recognize a person. What else do people and computers use? Are there some ways that people are better than computers at recognizing who a person is?

UNIT

THREE

Night scene of the central
business district of Singapore

CITIES

FOCUS

1. What are the largest cities in your country?

2. What is your favorite city? Why? Is it just a good place to visit, or is it also a good place to live?

Academic Vocabulary

a community	reliance	to restrict
an environment	a resident	a trend

Multiword Vocabulary

[handwritten: any place] *[handwritten: It's becoming more]*

anywhere in the world   more and more

city planning   public transportation

economic opportunities   traffic congestion

[handwritten: way to make money]   *[handwritten: heavy traffic, too many cars.]*

Reading Preview

A **Preview.** Read the title of Reading 1. Look at the photos on pages 46–49 and read their captions. Then check (✓) four topics that you think might be in this reading.

_____ **1.** Differences between older cities and newer cities

_____ **2.** Problems with driving in cities

_____ **3.** Life in small towns

_____ **4.** Types of people who move to cities

_____ **5.** Living in the countryside far from both cities and small towns

_____ **6.** Types of restaurants in big cities

_____ **7.** Quality of education in cities

B **Topic vocabulary.** The following words appear in Reading 1. Look at the words and answer the questions with a partner.

bikers	neighborhoods	surroundings
crime	pedestrians	traffic
historical sites	smoke	waterfront

1. Which words describe people who go from one place to another?

2. Which words are related to places you might find in a city or places people might live?

3. Which words are related to problems that cities often have?

C **Predict.** What do you think this reading will be about? Discuss each word in Exercise B and predict how it may relate to the reading.

What makes great cities? They are more than just places to work and play. Read about how today's city planners are trying to make cities great places to "live" in every sense of the word.

Livable Cities

A crowded bicycle stand in Amsterdam, Netherlands. Amsterdam is ranked as one of the best cities to live in the world.

LIVABLE CITIES

Downtown restaurants at night in Centre Ville, Beirut, Lebanon

1 It's midday in a typical major city almost anywhere in the world. You're standing on the corner, trying to cross the street. Buses, trucks, cars, and taxis go by. The noise of the traffic hurts your ears. Black smoke fills the air. It's dirty. It's noisy. It's dangerous. You came to this city because it was where you could find work, but do you really want to "live" here?

2 Urban planners[1] understand how you feel. They know that people want to work, play, and shop in an environment that has clean air, safe streets, and attractive surroundings. They are trying to solve some of these problems by creating "livable cities." There are two important ways to make cities more "livable"—encourage less use of private cars and build new types of neighborhoods.

3 To make cities more livable, many cities around the world are restricting car travel in certain areas. They are also creating some streets for pedestrians and bike riders only. When people walk and bike, the result is cleaner air to breathe and healthier and happier residents. Some major world cities that have streets for bikes only include Munich, Germany; Barcelona, Spain; and Paris, France. Many smaller cities have created streets like these, too.

4 In addition, some cities are charging drivers money to drive into the city. This money is called a "congestion fee." In Stockholm, Sweden; London, England; and Singapore, drivers must pay this fee to enter parts of the city. As a result, more people are carpooling[2] and taking public transportation. Fewer cars on the road means better air quality. It also means less traffic congestion. Congestion fees are working. In one month in Stockholm, there were 100,000 fewer cars on the road than there were the month before the city introduced the fee.

5 Another way to make cities livable is to design them so that people can live, shop, and work all

> "Another way to make cities livable is to design them so that people can live, shop, and work all in the same neighborhood."

in the same neighborhood. These neighborhoods are called "mixed-use" neighborhoods. Because people can work and shop near where they live, such neighborhoods also reduce residents' reliance on cars. These neighborhoods seem to have less crime, as well. As a result, many residents of mixed-use neighborhoods report that they have more peace of mind and feel less stressed.

6 One example of a mixed-use neighborhood is Atlantic Station in Atlanta, Georgia, USA. Atlantic Station opened in 2005. Homes, offices, shops, and entertainment are all within 138 acres. The residents can walk or bicycle almost anywhere, so they don't need cars to get around. There's also a special bus that connects them to Atlanta's public transportation system. The residents of Atlantic Station call their home a "live-work-play community."

7 Another example of a mixed-use neighborhood is Centre Ville, Beirut, Lebanon. Centre Ville is the result of a 25-year redevelopment plan

---

[1] *urban planners:* people who design and plan city areas

[2] *carpooling:* going places with friends or workers in one car together

for the waterfront city center. Urban planners designed a mixed-use area that preserves[3] ancient historical sites. The new design puts Byzantine mosaics, Roman baths, old city walls, and the remains of a Phoenician fort[4] in the same area as housing, business, and entertainment areas. One of the main features of Centre Ville is Star Square. In the evening, this area is filled with restaurant diners and families walking with their children.

More and more people around the world are moving into cities for the economic opportunities that cities provide and to improve their lives generally. As urban populations continue to grow, it becomes even more important for urban planners to design cities well. Current trends in city planning such as bike- and pedestrian-friendly streets and mixed-use neighborhoods are just two approaches to making cities healthy and more livable.

8

---

[3] *preserves:* keeps; protects
[4] *fort:* a building for soldiers where people can come to protect themselves from enemies

READING COMPREHENSION

Big Picture

A Read the following statements. Check (✓) the five statements that express the main ideas of Reading 1.

_____ **1.** Many big cities are not nice places to live in.

_____ **2.** Urban planners know that most people want safe streets and safe communities.

_____ **3.** Urban planners are trying to solve big city problems.

_____ **4.** Many cities use congestion fees to reduce the number of cars.

_____ **5.** Improving transportation is an urban planning goal.

_____ **6.** Neighborhoods with places for work, shopping, and living solve some urban problems.

_____ **7.** Atlantic Station opened in 2005.

_____ **8.** Centre Ville, Beirut, Lebanon, is an example of a mixed-use neighborhood.

B Every author has a purpose for writing a text. Read the list below and check (✓) the author's purpose for writing Reading 1.

_____ **1.** To persuade people to move out of cities

_____ **2.** To inform people how to make cities good places to live

_____ **3.** To explain how cities cause stress and illness

_____ **4.** To give examples of healthy cities

Close-Up

A Choose the answer that best completes each of the following sentences.

1. According to paragraph 1, many people move to cities to _____.
   a. get better jobs
   b. find cheaper housing
   c. have good public transportation

2. According to the reading, the two main ways to make cities more livable are _____.
   a. by creating shopping areas and by providing job opportunities near housing
   b. by reducing crime and by adding parks and green areas
   c. by improving city transportation and by creating a new type of neighborhood

3. Urban planners are creating more streets that only allow _____.
   a. people and bicycles
   b. public transportation
   c. private cars

4. According to paragraph 4, some cities are trying to reduce traffic congestion by _____.
   a. providing free buses
   b. charging extra fees for driving
   c. asking people to walk to work

5. An important feature of mixed-use neighborhoods is that people can _____ in the same area.
   a. work and live
   b. study and find restaurants
   c. get health care and education

6. According to paragraph 5, mixed-use neighborhoods have _____ than traditional neighborhoods.
   a. residents with less peace of mind
   b. fewer good job opportunities
   c. fewer cars and less crime

7. Atlantic Station and Centre Ville are examples of _____.
   a. neighborhoods that need improving
   b. communities with congestion fees
   c. mixed-use neighborhoods

8. An unusual feature of the new design of Centre Ville is that _____.
   a. people can eat and walk in Star Square
   b. historical sites exist next to shops and housing
   c. there are places for people to take baths and to sit on ancient walls

9. According to paragraph 8, it is important for urban planners to keep improving the design of cities because _____.
   a. more and more people don't have cars
   b. cities are continuing to get more crowded
   c. there are fewer and fewer job opportunities

B Compare answers to Exercise A with a partner or in a small group. If you don't agree, discuss your answers and try to agree on one correct answer.

Reading Skill

A Underline the cause-and-effect signal words in the following sentences from Reading 1. The first one is done for you.

1. You came to this city <u>because</u> it was where you could find work, but do you really want to "live" here? (Par. 1)

2. When people walk and bike, <u>the result</u> is cleaner air to breathe and healthier and happier residents. (Par. 3)

3. In Stockholm, Sweden; London, England; and Singapore, drivers must pay this fee to enter parts of the city. <u>As a result</u>, more people are carpooling and taking public transportation. (Par. 4)

4. These neighborhoods seem to have less crime, as well. <u>As a result</u>, many residents of mixed-use neighborhoods report that they have more peace of mind and feel less stressed. (Par. 5)

5. The residents can walk or bicycle almost anywhere, <u>so</u> they don't need cars to get around. (Par. 6)

B Work with a partner. Read the sentences in Exercise A. Identify the causes and the effects in each sentence or pair of sentences. List them in the chart below.

Causes	Effects
1. *looking for work*	*came to the city*
2.	
3.	
4.	
5.	

VOCABULARY PRACTICE

Academic Vocabulary

A Find the words in bold in Reading 1. Use the context to help you match sentence parts to create definitions.

1. The **environment** (Par. 2) is _a_ .
2. **Restricting** (Par. 3) something is _d_ .
3. The **residents** (Par. 3) of a house or an area are _e_ .
4. **Reliance** (Par. 5) is _f_ .
5. A **community** (Par. 6) is _b_ .
6. **Trends** (Par. 8) are _c_ .

a. everything in the world around you including the air, land, and sea
b. a group of people who live in the same area and often share the same interests
c. new, fashionable ways of doing things
d. stopping it from becoming too large
e. the people who live in it
f. your need for something

B Choose an academic word from Exercise A to complete each of the following sentences. Notice and learn the words in bold because they often appear with the academic words.

1. You can't drive into some parts of Golden Gate Park in San Francisco on certain days. The city is _Restricting_ **access** to the park on Sunday afternoons.
2. Some parents think that a big city is an **unhealthy** _enviroment_ for a child, but I disagree. There are many educational and cultural opportunities for kids who live in cities.
3. Some **current** _trend_ in city high schools include new uses of technology and even the use of students' cell phones in class.
4. Jana is an important **member of the** _Community_. She has been mayor twice, and now she is the head of the police department.
5. Some countries are trying to use more alternative sources of energy to reduce their _Reliance_ **on** oil.
6. Local _Residence_ can use the city swimming pool for free, but people who don't live here must pay a fee.

Multiword Vocabulary

A Find the multiword vocabulary in bold in Reading 1. Use the context to help you understand the meaning. Then match each item to the correct definition.

1. **anywhere in the world** (Par. 1) _d_
2. **traffic congestion** (Par. 4) _e_
3. **public transportation** (Par. 4) _a_
4. **more and more** (Par. 8) _b_
5. **economic opportunities** (Par. 8) _c_
6. **city planning** (Par. 8) _f_

a. buses and trains
b. in growing numbers
c. chances to make money
d. in every country
e. too many cars and trucks using the streets
f. decisions about where to put streets, houses, businesses, etc.

ACHery → FLectte.

B Complete the following sentences with the correct multiword vocabulary from Exercise A.

1. Evan uses ___*Public transfer*___ instead of driving a car because he wants to live in a place with clean air.

2. The population of San Diego grew quickly, and city planners did not build enough new roads for all the new people. As a result, there is a lot of ___*traffic conges*___ on the freeways.

3. Marta is interested in ways to improve neighborhoods, so she is going to go to college to study ___*City Planning*___.

4. ___*move and move*___ people want to live in cities every year. In fact, according to the World Bank, 60 percent of all people will live in cities by 2030.

5. If I could live ___*anywhere in the world*___, I would live in Paris.

6. If you need a good job and want to find ways to make money, you should move to a big city. That's where all the ___*economic opportun*___ are.

Use the Vocabulary

Write answers to the following questions. Use the words in bold in your answers. Then share your answers with a partner.

1. If you could live **anywhere in the world**, where would you live?

2. What kinds of **public transportation** do you have in your **community**?

3. What kinds of **economic opportunities** are there where you live?

4. What are solutions to **traffic congestion** in some major cities that you know about?

5. Do people in your area have a great **reliance on** cars? If yes, is it possible to change this behavior? How?

6. What are some **current trends** among young people where you live?

THINK AND DISCUSS

Work in a small group. Use the information in the reading and your own ideas to discuss the following questions.

1. **Express an opinion.** Reading 1 mentions some cities with "congestion fees." Do you think fees like these are a good idea? Why, or why not?

2. **Discuss problems and solutions.** Do mixed-use neighborhoods sound like a good solution to some of the problems that cities have? Why, or why not?

3. **Apply your knowledge.** Think of a city you are familiar with. What are some ways that would make it a better place to live?

Academic Vocabulary

[handwritten: to buld] *[handwritten: make a plan]*

to construct   distinctive *[handwritten: seperate]*   income *[handwritten: money you make from job]*

to design   diverse *[handwritten: varied]*   a route *[handwritten: a way to go, a road]*

[handwritten: Many ≠ things]

Multiword Vocabulary

[handwritten: to be a symbol]

to be symbolic of   to make a decision *[handwritten: to decide]*

to have a vision *[handwritten: have a Idea]*   a sense of unity *[handwritten: a feeling of being together]*

a large number of *[handwritten: many]*   to succeed in

[handwritten: to do Something well]

[handwritten: ⊚ A feeling of being united as one group.]

Reading Preview

A **Preview.** Skim Reading 2 by reading the first sentence and last sentence of each paragraph. Then check (✓) four topics below that you think might be in this reading.

_____ **1.** The leader of Kazakhstan's ideas for his new country

_____ **2.** Public transportation in the capital city of Kazakhstan

_____ **3.** Fashion trends among young people in today's Kazakhstan

_____ **4.** Symbolism of the buildings of the capital city of Kazakhstan

_____ **5.** Traditions and customs of the Kazakh people

_____ **6.** The design of Astana's new buildings

B **Topic Vocabulary.** The following words appear in Reading 2. Look at the words and answer the questions with a partner.

architect *[2]*   futuristic *[1]*   shopping mall *[3]*

beach *[3]*   inspiring *[1]*   structure *[3]*

builder *[2]*   leader *[2]*   wealthy *[1]* *(rich)*

capital *[3]*   monument *[3]*

1. Which words are adjectives? What do they mean?

2. Which words relate to people? *[2]*

3. Which words are places? *[3]*

C **Predict.** What do you think this reading will be about? Discuss each word in Exercise B and predict how it may relate to the reading.

Enter Astana, one of the world's newest and most modern cities. Read about its location, its unusual public spaces, and Nursultan Nazarbayev, the man who made it happen.

The Baiterek Tower in Astana, Kazakhstan

Kazakhstan's City of
TOMORROW

In 1991, Kazakhstan was a new country with a large number of problems. It was also an extremely diverse country with 131 different ethnicities.[1] Nursultan Nazarbayev, the new leader of Kazakhstan, knew he needed to do something to give the people of his country a sense of unity. Nazarbayev made a decision. He decided to build a futuristic city and to move the capital there.

The original Kazakh capital, Almaty, was a pleasant city with beautiful mountain scenery and a relatively mild climate. Many people were surprised that Nazarbayev wanted to move the capital to a faraway place where the landscape was flat and the weather was extreme. But Nazarbayev was a determined man. He had a vision of a city full of unique and inspiring buildings. Kazakhstan's oil was producing a great deal of income for the country, and Nazarbayev wanted the architecture to reflect his vision of a wealthy and important new country. He started building the new

> *"Today, this unique futuristic city is home to 700,000 people."*

capital, Astana, in 1997, just six years after the birth of his nation. Ambitious young Kazakhs started to arrive soon after. Today, this unique futuristic city is home to 700,000 people.

One building in Astana that is symbolic of Nazarbayev's vision for the future is the Baiterek. Nazarbayev designed the building himself. People say he made a sketch of the building on a paper napkin and then gave it to architects and builders to construct. The Baiterek is a 318-foot (97-meter) tower in the city center. It's a treelike structure with a golden glass ball at the top. The monument represents a Kazakh myth.[2] According to the myth, Samruk—a bird—laid a golden egg in the top of a tree every year. The tree is symbolic of life, and the golden egg is symbolic of the sun. The building therefore symbolizes a new beginning and a great future for Kazakhstan.

When Nazarbayev decided to build a huge pyramid in Astana, he talked to

---

[1] *ethnicities:* groups of people who have different cultural backgrounds and traditions

[2] *myth:* a story that is not true, but that may have great meaning for some people

The Palace of Peace and Reconciliation, Astana

БЕЙБІТШІЛІК ЖӘНЕ КЕЛІСІМ САРАЙЫ

Figure 1. Kazakhstan: Major Cities and Resources

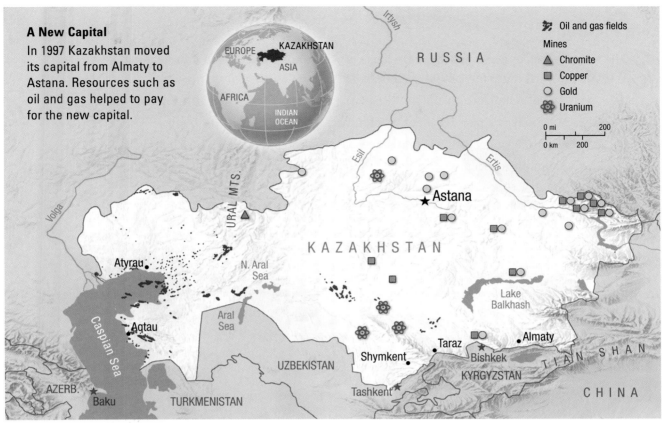

A New Capital

In 1997 Kazakhstan moved its capital from Almaty to Astana. Resources such as oil and gas helped to pay for the new capital.

Oil and gas fields
Mines
△ Chromite
□ Copper
○ Gold
⚛ Uranium

0 mi   200
0 km   200

Source: National Geographic Magazine, February 2012

world-famous architects. Finally, he chose Norman Foster, a British architect. The pyramid, called the Palace of Peace and Reconciliation, is 252 feet (77 meters) high, and it cost 58 billion dollars to construct. The futuristic structure is a meeting place and a spiritual center. Its design represents all religions of the world.

Foster also designed a distinctive shopping mall in Astana called the Khan Shatyr. The Khan Shatyr looks like a giant tent. It's a 490-feet (150-meter) high structure made of steel and glass. It took three and a half years and four hundred million dollars to build. A man-made river runs through the center of the Khan Shatyr. There is an indoor beach with white sand that comes from the faraway Maldives Islands. The glass structure lets in sunlight, and cooling and heating systems keep year-round temperatures between 59°F and 86°F (15°C and 30°C).

Astana continues to develop. In 2010, the city held a competition for a design for a green

mixed-use neighborhood. An Italian architecture firm won the competition with their design "Solid Waves." Solid Waves combines commercial and residential buildings with green public spaces. In addition, Nazarbayev saw the need for a good public transportation system. Although there are many bus, trolley, and public minibus routes, Nazarbayev planned a light-rail system[3] for Astana.

Nazarbayev's new city is not popular with everyone in Kazakhstan. Some people complain that it wasted national resources. They also complain that Nazarbayev created Astana as a symbol of his power. But the city has succeeded in attracting many businesses. As a result, young people continue to flood in to Astana. As a recent arrival said, "I know that in the future I will be very wealthy. It's a really lucky place for me."

---

[3] *light-rail system:* system of small trains that run through a city

READING COMPREHENSION

Big Picture

A The following statements are the main ideas of paragraphs 1, 2, 3, and 6 in Reading 2. Write the correct paragraph number next to its main idea.

3 **1.** One of Astana's unusual buildings, the Baiterek, is symbolic of a Kazakh myth.

2 **2.** Nazarbayev's plan for a new capital became a reality.

1 **3.** Nazarbayev decided to build a new futuristic capital city for his country.

6 **4.** Astana features modern trends in city planning such as mixed-use neighborhoods.

B Compare answers to Exercise A with a partner. Then complete the main ideas of the paragraphs below.

Paragraph 4: A famous British architect designed _the Palace of Peace and_

Paragraph 5: The _Khan Shatyv_ is an unusual shopping mall.

Paragraph 7: Although some people _complain_ about the building of Astana, young people and businesses _move flood_ into the city.

Close-Up

A Decide which of the following statements are true or false according to the reading. Write *T* (True) or *F* (False) next to each one.

T **1.** There are more than 100 different ethnicities in Kazakhstan.

T **2.** The name of the old capital of Kazakhstan is Almaty.

F **3.** Nazarbayev moved the capital to a place that has a good climate.

F **4.** All Kazakhs thought that moving the capital was a good idea.

T **5.** The idea for the Baiterek tower came from Nazarbayev.

F **6.** The Baiterek looks like a pyramid.

F **7.** It cost 58 million dollars to build the Palace of Peace and Reconciliation.

T **8.** A British architect designed and built the Palace of Peace and Reconciliation.

T **9.** The Khan Shatyr contains a beach.

F **10.** "Solid Waves" is the name of a building in Astana.

B Work with a partner or in a small group. Change the false statements in Exercise A to make them true.

Reading Skill

A Read the following sentences from Reading 2. Each sentence is followed by two statements. Choose the statement that is the best inference for the sentence from the reading.

1. It was also an extremely diverse country with 131 different ethnicities. Nursultan Nazarbayev, the new leader of Kazakhstan, knew he needed to do something to give the people of his country a sense of unity. (Par. 1)
   a. Nazarbayev was worried that the different ethnicities would want to leave Kazakhstan.
   b. Nazarbayev was worried that the different ethnicities would not get along well with each other.

2. The original Kazakh capital, Almaty, was a pleasant city with beautiful mountain scenery and a relatively mild climate. Many people were surprised that Nazarbayev wanted to move the capital to a faraway place where the landscape was flat and the weather was extreme. (Par. 2)
   a. The weather in Astana was similar to the weather of the old capital.
   b. The weather in Astana was not as good as the weather in the old capital.

3. Many people were surprised that Nazarbayev wanted to move the capital to a faraway place where the landscape was flat and the weather was extreme. But Nazarbayev was a determined man. (Par. 2)
   a. Many people weren't sure that Nazarbayev's idea was a good idea.
   b. Many people were excited about Nazarbayev's idea.

4. Ambitious young Kazakhs started to arrive soon after. (Par. 2)
   a. Kazakhs came to Astana because they were looking for a new place to live.
   b. Kazakhs came to Astana because they thought there were good job opportunities there.

5. When Nazarbayev decided to build a huge pyramid in Astana, he talked to many world-famous architects. Finally, he chose Norman Foster, a British architect. (Par. 4)
   a. Norman Foster is a well-known architect.
   b. Norman Foster is a friend of Nazarbayev's.

6. As a result, young people continue to flood in to Astana. As a recent arrival said, "I know that in the future I will be very wealthy. It's a really lucky place for me." (Par. 7)
   a. Young Kazakhs still see Astana as a place of opportunity.
   b. Young Kazakhs care too much about being wealthy.

B Compare answers to Exercise A with a partner.

VOCABULARY PRACTICE

Academic Vocabulary

A Find the words in bold in Reading 2. Use the context and the sentences below to match each word to its correct definition.

_d_ **1.** The United States is called a melting pot because of its **diverse** (Par. 1) immigrant population.

_a_ **2.** Usually when people change their jobs, their **income** (Par. 2) changes, too.

_c_ **3.** An architecture firm in Singapore **designed** (Par. 3) the building that won the annual competition.

_e_ **4.** Most builders follow detailed plans when they **construct** (Par. 3) buildings.

_f_ **5.** Certain buildings in Barcelona have a **distinctive** (Par. 5) style. They don't look like buildings in any other city in the world.

_b_ **6.** The fastest **routes** (Par. 6) are the highways. But you can also take the smaller roads that are prettier, but slower.

a. money you get for working or selling something

b. ways to get to specific places

c. drew a picture and made plans

d. varied; different in many ways

e. build; make; create

f. having a special quality that is easy to notice

B The words in bold show academic words from Exercise A and words they often appear with. Match the word combination on the left with a phrase on the right that is similar in meaning.

_b_ **1. a diverse population**   **a.** a special characteristic

_a_ **2. a distinctive feature**   **b.** a variety of people

_e_ **3. a large income**   **c.** make a way to do something

_f_ **4. design a building**   **d.** short ways to get somewhere

_c_ **5. construct a plan**   **e.** a big amount of money

_d_ **6. direct routes**   **f.** plan a structure

Multiword Vocabulary

A Find the words in the box below in Reading 2. Use the context and the words in parentheses to help you understand the meaning. Then complete the sentences with the multiword vocabulary.

a large number of (Par. 1)	made a decision (Par. 1)	is symbolic of (Par. 3)
a sense of unity (Par. 1)	had a vision (Par. 2)	succeeded in (Par. 7)

1. Nazarbayev _had a vision_ (had an idea in one's mind) of a new country that was very futuristic.

2. Nazarbayev _made a decision_ (chose what to do) to move the capital, which surprised many people.

3. Nazarbayev _succeeded in_ (was able to) getting famous architects to design buildings for Astana.

The Kahn Shatyr shopping
mall in Astana

4. _____A Large number of_____ (many) young people have moved to Astana already.

5. The Baiterek _____is symbolic of_____ (represents) an important Kazakh myth.

6. Nazarbayev knew he needed to create _____Sense of unity._____ (a feeling of belonging to a group) for the people of his new country because there are many different ethnic groups.

B Compare answers to Exercise A with a partner.

Use the Vocabulary

Write answers to the following questions. Use the words in bold in your answers. Then share your answers with a partner.

1. Which groups of people do you feel **a sense of unity** with? Give reasons for your answer.

2. What is an important **decision** that you have **made** recently? Was the **decision** easy or hard **to make**? Why?

3. Do you **have a vision** for your future or for the future of your children? Describe it.

4. Think of a building in your area that has a **distinctive style**. What makes it distinctive?

5. If you could **design** your dream home, what would it be like?

6. What **routes** can you take to school? Which is the **fastest route**? Which route do you take? Why?

7. Is your community **diverse**? If so, describe what makes it diverse.

THINK AND DISCUSS

Work in a small group. Use the information in the reading and your own ideas to discuss the following questions.

1. **Give an opinion.** What do you think of Nazarbayev? Do you think he is popular in his country? Can you think of reasons that some Kazakh people might not like him?

2. **Understand causes and effects.** What were Nazarbayev's goals in building Astana? Do you think he succeeded?

3. **Apply what you learned.** How is Astana similar to or different from another city you are familiar with?

Celebration, Florida, USA

Vocabulary Review

A Complete the paragraphs with the vocabulary below that you have studied in the unit.

6 city planning
4 design the buildings
distinctive features 5
2 had a vision

a large number of 3
members of the community 1
reliance on 7
traffic congestion 8

    Celebration, Florida, is a small town near Disneyland. Most of the people who live there love it. But Celebration isn't for everyone. Some

_____ complain that it feels
         1

artificial—like it actually belongs in Disneyland. There's a good reason for this. In the early 1990s,

the Walt Disney Company _____. They wanted to create a town that
             2

reminded people of a safe, small American town from before the 1940s. They contacted

_____ world-famous architects to help them _____. They
         3   4

told them to give each public building _____ so that the post office, the bank,
                            5

and the city hall would all look very different. They also told the architects to make the homes

look like traditional homes from different parts of the United States.

    Another important idea in the _____ was to make it so that people could
                                 6

walk everywhere, so housing and shopping areas are all within walking distance. As a result, the

residents don't have a _____ cars, and there is never any
                            7

_____.
    8

B Compare answers to Exercise A with a partner. Then discuss the following question.

Does Celebration sound like a nice place to live? Why, or why not?

C Complete the following sentences in a way that shows that you understand the meaning of the words in bold.

1. It's a good idea to **restrict car use** in big cities because ___our reliance on car *prevents us from exercising*___.

2. My idea of a good **study environment** is one that is/has ___minimal interruptions.___

3. In the next 20 years or so, there will probably be **more and more** _____.

4. Often the things that **are** the most **symbolic of** a person's childhood are _____.

D Work with a partner and write four sentences that include any four of the vocabulary items below. You may use any verb tense and make nouns plural if you want.

anywhere in the world
current trends

diverse population
economic opportunities

resident of
succeed in

Connect the Readings

A Look back at Readings 1 and 2 to complete the chart below. Put a check (✓) in the boxes to show which topics appeared in each reading. Note that some topics appeared in both readings.

	Reading 1	Reading 2
1. Symbolic structures		
2. Mixed-use neighborhoods		
3. Modern architecture		
4. Job opportunities for new residents		
5. Fixing environmental problems		
6. Weather		
7. Public transportation		
8. The cost of the buildings		

B With a partner or in a small group, compare answers to Exercise A. Then discuss the following questions.

1. If a topic appeared in both readings, in which reading do you think that topic was more important? Why?

2. Of all of the topics listed in Exercise A, which was the most interesting to you? Why?

C Discuss the following questions with a partner. Use your understanding of the readings and your own ideas.

1. What did you learn in this unit about new trends in planning cities?

2. Describe a mixed-use neighborhood that you know about. What advantages does it have?

3. Think about the public transportation where you live. What would you do to improve it?

4. What do you think cities will be like 50 years from now?

A young girl on a hammock watches a movie on a tablet computer in Thailand.

FOCUS

1. What electronic devices do you use every day? Which one do you use the most?

2. What are some ways technology has changed your life in the last five years?

Technology

READING 1

Academic Vocabulary

Handwritten: Permission to use — a way to enter — make bigger — to Explain — Something — Complicated — Defend on somethink — You share something — to do Surgery — to Look Into the Future to make a plan — easy to get — Everyone Know is True — Something that bothers you

access   to expand   an item

complex   to illustrate   to project

Multiword Vocabulary

to be addicted to   readily available

to have something in   there is no question

common   that

to perform an operation   a valid concern

We can use smart phones to help us find out almost anything. But soon, we won't need our phones for this purpose. Learn about a new technology that will change the way we see our world.

Reading Preview

A **Preview.** Skim Reading 1. Then check (✓) three topics below that you think might be in this reading.

_____ **1.** The history of the Internet

_____ **2.** The future of cell phone technology

_____ **3.** The ability to see computer-generated information when you look at things

_____ **4.** The problems of having too much information

_____ **5.** A new technology that changes the way we see reality

_____ **6.** Becoming dependent on our cell phones

B **Topic vocabulary.** The following words appear in Reading 1. Look at the words and answer the questions with a partner.

1 apps   *2* menu   *1* screen

1 cell phone   *3* patients   travel guide

1 computer-generated   *2* reviews   *2* videos

3 doctors

1. Which words most closely relate to technology?

2. Which words describe places where you can get information?

3. Which words are connected in some way to the field of medicine?

C **Predict.** What do you think this reading will be about? Discuss each word in Exercise B and predict how it may relate to the reading.

A man wearing futuristic glasses. This wearable computer lets people access the internet, make calls, and take photos through spoken commands.

66 UNIT FOUR *Technology*

Augmented
REALITY

Y ou've just arrived at a party, but you 1 don't see anyone you know. Who should you talk to? You put on a special pair of glasses and look at the people again. Now, when you look around, you see information about each person on their faces or chests. You see the job each person has. You also see each person's interests. You can even see the friends you have in common. As you look around, you notice someone who knows several of your friends, likes the same kind of music as you, and also loves to cook. You approach this person.

"Augmented reality, or AR, adds pictures, sounds, text, and other types of information to the real world."

Can you buy these special glasses right now? 2 No, not quite yet. But a technology called *augmented reality* may make them readily available soon. What is augmented reality? *Augment* means to "add to something or expand something." So, augmented reality is an expanded reality. Augmented reality, or AR, adds pictures, sounds, text, and other types of information to the real world. This extra information comes from computer software.

Some forms of AR are already in use. You 3 can see them on television. For example, when you watch a sport such as soccer, you can see the score and the amount of playing time on the TV screen. In addition, the TV producers often draw circles or lines on the TV screen to more clearly illustrate something. This is a simple kind of AR that has been around for many years. Doctors use a more complex type of AR. For example, they can project an MRI[1] scan of a person's head onto the head itself. Then, while they are performing an operation, the doctors can look at the MRI scan on the patient's head. Doctors can also project videos of complicated operations onto their patients' bodies. The video shows them what to do next.

AR is not just for television, doctors, or other 4 professionals. Many AR applications—software

---

[1] *MRI (magnetic resonance imaging):* a picture of the soft parts inside a person's body

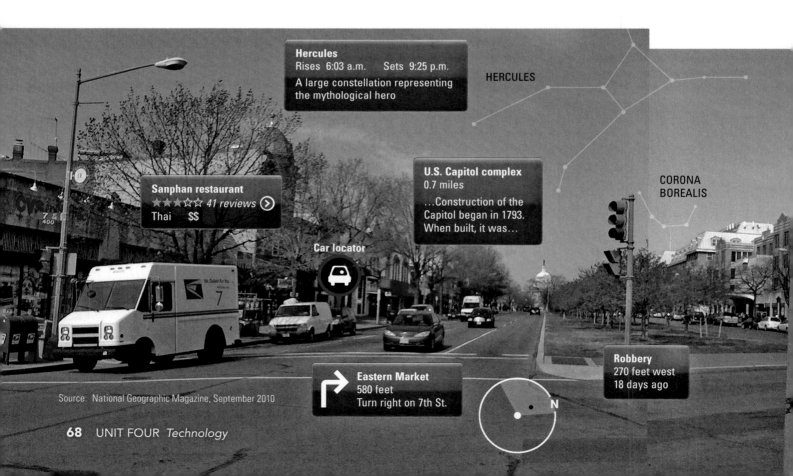

Hercules
Rises 6:03 a.m.   Sets 9:25 p.m.
A large constellation representing the mythological hero

HERCULES

Sanphan restaurant
★★★☆☆ *41 reviews* ⊙
Thai $$

U.S. Capitol complex
0.7 miles
...Construction of the Capitol began in 1793. When built, it was...

CORONA BOREALIS

Car locator

Eastern Market
580 feet
Turn right on 7th St.

Robbery
270 feet west
18 days ago

Source: National Geographic Magazine, September 2010

programs—already exist for smartphones. Smartphone AR uses your phone's GPS software, so it knows where you are. Based on your location, the application, or app, can connect to and then show you information about nearby places and objects that have already been entered into a database. For example, imagine you're walking down the street trying to decide where to eat. There's an application for that. Just hold your phone up to a street with restaurants and your phone will show you reviews, menu items, and prices—already entered into a database—in front of the restaurants you see. Have you ever lost your car in a parking lot? There's an AR app for that! Just get out of your car and take a picture. Later, the AR application on your phone will use GPS to direct you back to your car. Are you interested in the stars? Hold your phone up to the sky. You will see the names of the stars. You can also see the names of the constellations.[2] There's an app for that, too.

Many other useful AR apps are already in use on smartphones. Travelers can use AR apps instead of carrying around a guidebook or hiring 5

a travel guide. When you are traveling, just point your phone at something to get information about it. For example, point your phone at the Eiffel Tower and read its height, age, and admission price on the screen. There are AR apps for shoppers, too. Point your phone at an item in a store, for example, and get information on the price and quality. You can even get information on the same product at other stores.

In the future, we probably won't use cell 6 phone screens to see augmented reality. A pair of glasses or contact lenses[3] might be all we need. This is an exciting idea, but there are some concerns. Some people worry that AR might produce too much information. Sometimes, too much information can be confusing. Others worry that people might get to be addicted to seeing reality through AR apps. They think people might come to prefer augmented reality to actual reality. These may be valid concerns. However, there is no question that AR is here to stay. Soon, everyone will have access to it and people will learn to get used to it.

---

[2] *constellations:* groups of stars that form a pattern

[3] *contact lenses:* small plastic lenses that go on the surface of the eyes to improve eyesight

622-624 North Carolina Ave. SE
900 feet
List price: $2,995,000
Bed: 7   Bath: 8
On market: 420 days

Peregrine Espresso
195 feet
Free Wi-Fi

flickr: Eastern Market Fire
510 feet
Taken: 2007-04-30
9:35:35 a.m.

Bus stop
70 feet
Nearest for
32 34 36
A11 C40
CIRC

Subway stop
140 feet
Nearest for
● Orange Line
● Blue Line

READING COMPREHENSION

Big Picture

A Below are the topics of each paragraph in Reading 1. Number them in the order in which they appear in the reading.

_____ **a.** An explanation of the meaning of the term *augmented reality*

_____ **b.** The possible future of augmented reality

_____ **c.** Current uses of augmented reality for tourists and shoppers

_____ **d.** An example of a person using augmented reality at a party

_____ **e.** Current uses of augmented reality on TV and in hospitals

_____ **f.** Current uses of augmented reality on smartphones

B Compare answers to Exercise A with a partner. Then discuss what you think the main idea of the whole reading is.

Close-Up

A Choose the word or phrase in parentheses that correctly completes each sentence.

1. According to the reading, what happens at the party in paragraph 1 (is / is not) possible now.

2. According to paragraph 2, augmented reality allows you to see (information about / what's inside) the things in front of you.

3. According to paragraph 3, television producers already use augmented reality for (drama / sports) programs.

4. Doctors are (already / not yet) able to see projected videos on their patients.

5. According to paragraph 4, smartphone-based AR (needs / does not need) to know your location in order to work.

6. According to paragraphs 4 and 5, smartphone applications use augmented reality for (mainly practical / mainly entertainment) purposes already.

7. Augmented reality applications on smartphones (can already / cannot yet) replace guidebooks for tourists and travelers.

8. So far, most personal use of augmented reality is only (through special glasses / on a smartphone screen).

9. Some people wonder if augmented reality will cause problems because (people might use it too often / it might be bad for your eyes).

10. According to the reading, we (will / will not) probably all have access to augmented reality very soon.

B Compare answers to Exercise A with a partner. If you don't agree, find statements in Reading 1 that support your answers.

Reading Skill

Connecting Examples to the Main Ideas They Support

Writers often use examples to support their main ideas. Examples help the reader to understand the main points a writer is trying to make. Writers often signal that they are providing an example to support a main idea by using signal words and phrases. These include *for example, such as, for instance,* and *like.* Good readers look for these signal words and phrases to help them find examples so they can better understand the main ideas of a reading.

Notice how the example below helps to clarify the writer's main idea.

Some forms of AR are already in use. You can see them on television. For example, when you watch a sport such as soccer, you can see the score . . .

In the sentence above, *For example* signals the example. However, not all example sentences use signal words. Notice how there are no signal words in the second sentence below to show that it is providing a supporting example for the main idea before it.

Many other useful AR applications are already in use on smartphones. Travelers can use AR applications instead of carrying around a guidebook or hiring a travel guide.

A Read the examples in the chart below. Find the missing ideas the examples support in Reading 1. Write the main ideas in the chart.

Main Ideas	Examples
1. *You see information about each person on their faces or chests.*	You see the job each person has. (Par. 1)
2.	For example, they [doctors] can project an MRI scan of a person's head onto the head itself. (Par. 3)
3.	Just get out of your car and take a picture. Later, the AR application on your phone will use GPS to direct you back to your car. (Par. 4)
4.	For example, point your phone at the Eiffel Tower and read its height, age, and admission price on the screen. (Par. 5)
5.	Point your phone at an item in a store, for example, and get information on the price and quality. (Par. 5)

B Scan the reading for more examples that support the main ideas that you found in Exercise A. Then compare your answers with a partner.

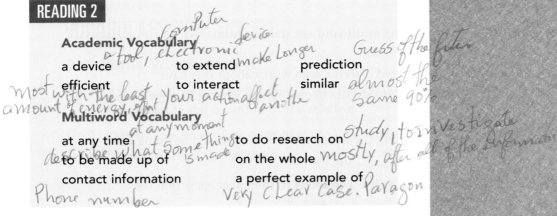

READING 2

Academic Vocabulary

Computer

a device *a tool, electronic device*   to extend *make longer*   prediction *Guess of the future*

efficient *Most with the least amount of energy, effort*   to interact *Your action affect another*   similar *almost the Same 90%*

Multiword Vocabulary   *at any moment*

at any time   *describe what something* to do research on *Study, to investigate*

to be made up of *is made*   on the whole *mostly, after all of the information*

contact information   a perfect example of *Very clear Case. Paragon*

Phone number

Reading Preview

A **Preview.** Read the title of Reading 2. Look at the photos on pages 74–77 and read their captions. Then discuss the following questions with a partner or in a small group.

1. What do you think a *cyborg* might be?
2. How do you think someone controls a bionic hand?
3. What is an anthropologist?

B **Topic vocabulary.** The following words appear in Reading 2. Look at the words and answer the questions with a partner.

1 digital   mechanical   *1* post
1 electronic   *3* negative   *1* site
2 hammer   *3* positive   *1* text
3 improve

1. Which words are connected to using social media or the Internet?
2. Which words relate to machines and tools?
3. Which words are about things being good or bad?

C **Predict.** What do you think this reading will be about? Discuss each word in Exercise B and predict how it may relate to the reading.

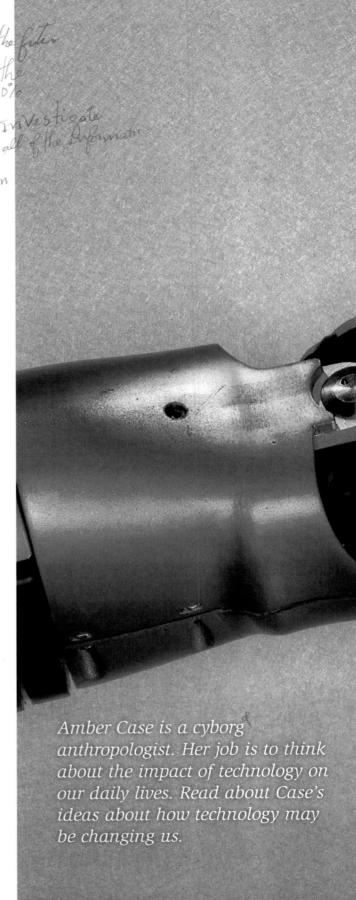

Amber Case is a cyborg anthropologist. Her job is to think about the impact of technology on our daily lives. Read about Case's ideas about how technology may be changing us.

From Humans to CYBORGS?

A bionic hand allows users to pick up very small objects with great accuracy.

Amber Case,
cyborg anthropologist

W hat happens if you lose your cell phone? Suddenly, you can't text your friends or post an update on a social networking site. Do you feel like a part of you is missing? Many people would say, "Yes!" This worries some people. They think people may be placing too much importance on objects such as phones. Amber Case thinks differently. She says that our devices have almost become a part of ourselves. She believes our devices are turning us into *cyborgs*, or human beings with mechanical and electronic body parts. Case is an anthropologist—a scientist who studies people and their relationships with the things that they use, such as tools. Case calls herself a *cyborg anthropologist*. She does research on how we interact with modern tools and how these tools are changing us and our way of life.

Our modern technological tools are very different from the types of tools that humans developed in the past. In the past, people invented tools such as the wheel and hammers. These tools made it possible for us to have more power and control over our physical world. As Case puts it, they extended our physical self. "Today's technology," Case says, "extends our mental self." Case says cell phones are a perfect example of this. Cell phones turn us into cyborgs, Case says, because they act like extensions of our brains. For example, a cell phone can hold our friends' contact information, so we don't have to memorize it. It is not surprising then that when we lose our cell phones, we panic because we feel like we have lost a part of our memory.

Case is particularly interested in how another modern tool—the Internet—is affecting us. Case points out that many people today have a digital self in addition to their real-world self. Your digital self is made up of all the bits of information about you that are online. Because of your digital self, people can get to know you even though they never meet you face-to-face. Case points out that just like in the real world, how you appear online can be very important. The result? Now people have to think carefully about how they present themselves in two worlds: the online world and the real world.

A SHORT HISTORY OF THE CELL PHONE

Martin Cooper invented the cell phone in the early 1970s. He made the first cell phone call in New York City on April 3, 1973. His phone weighed 2 pounds (0.9 kilos). It was about the size of a small loaf of bread. It was another nine years before cell phones became available to the public. By 1990, there were a million cell phone users worldwide and by 2013, there were six billion cell phones in use. Surprisingly, according to a World Bank report, cell phone use in developing countries grew faster than in developed areas. This may be because the developing world had a greater need for cell phones. In developing countries, people use cell phones for education and economic improvement. On the other hand, cell phone users in developed areas use cell phones mainly for communication, entertainment, and for checking the time.

Martin Cooper with an early cell phone

Case believes our relationship with technology is, on the whole, a positive thing. She believes that modern technology allows us actually to be more human because it helps us connect with each other. We can communicate with each other from anywhere and at any time. It also allows us to communicate easily with networks of people who have similar needs and interests. For example, if you are a student who needs help with homework, you can find that help online. There are also online communities for parents who are raising children with unusual diseases.

Does Case think our cyborg devices are 5 having a negative effect, too? As an anthropologist, Case knows we have these tools for a reason.

They fulfill specific needs. In today's world, we increasingly need access to information. As a result, Case notes, people are constantly checking their devices for messages and information. This helps us in many ways, but there could be some negative effects. Case does worry that many of us have less time to just think quietly.

Case makes the prediction that devices in 6 the future will continue to get more efficient at collecting and analyzing information. This will help us to do many things more efficiently and improve our daily lives in many ways. Technology, Case believes, will continue to extend our bodies and our minds and make life better for everyone.

READING COMPREHENSION

Big Picture

A The following statements are the main ideas of each paragraph in Reading 2. Write the correct paragraph number next to its main idea.

5 **1.** One negative effect of modern technology could be that we don't have much time to think quietly, according to Case.

2 **2.** A cell phone is a good example of how modern tools are like parts of our body.

6 **3.** Technology will continue to improve our lives, Case believes.

1 **4.** Amber Case is interested in how modern tools are affecting us.

4 **5.** Modern technology helps us to connect with other people.

3 **6.** The Internet is changing the way we present ourselves to others.

B Compare answers to Exercise A with a partner. Then discuss what you think the main idea is of the short extra reading, "A Short History of the Cell Phone," on page 77.

Close-Up

A Choose the answer that best completes each of the following sentences.

1. Cyborgs are mainly __*a*__ .
    a. people   **b.** machines

2. Amber Case studies __*a*__ .
    a. our relationships with tools   **b.** our relationships with cyborgs

3. According to Case, cell phones are an example of how modern technology can extend our __*b*__ .
    a. bodies   **b.** minds

4. Your __*b*__ is information about you that exists in the online world.
    a. real-world self   **b.** digital self

5. The reading uses online communities to give an example of how modern technology can __*a*__ .
    a. help us to connect with others   **b.** keep us from thinking

6. Amber Case has mainly __*b*__ feelings about modern technology.
    a. negative   **b.** positive

7. Amber Case would probably agree with the statement that __*b*__ .
    a. new technology creates too many new problems
    b. new technology will continue to solve problems

8. According to "A Short History of the Cell Phone," people in the developing world __*b*__ .
    a. mostly need cell phones to entertain themselves
    b. mostly need cell phones to improve their lives

B Compare answers to Exercise A with a partner. If you don't agree, find statements in Reading 2 and "A Short History of the Cell Phone" that support your answers.

Reading Skill

Identifying the Meaning of Unfamiliar Words

You can often identify the meaning of an unfamiliar word or phrase if you look at the **context** (the words and sentences around it). The context will have clues that could include an **explanation**, an **example**, or even a **definition** of the word.

Explanation

   Michael Wesch is worried that we already take technology for granted. It is so much a part of our daily lives that we expect it to always be there.

   To take (something) for granted means you accept something as normal without really thinking about it. The second sentence **explains** the expression.

Example

Michael Wesch, an anthropology professor at Kansas State University, studies our relationships with <u>cyberspace</u>. He is particularly interested in social networks and in how the Internet is changing the way we communicate.

Cyberspace refers to networks that allow people to communicate using computers. "Social networks" is an **example** of cyberspace, and the word "Internet" in the second sentence gives you another clue.

Definition

<u>*Anthropology*</u> *is the study of humanity, for example, human relationships, human societies, and how humans behave in different situations.*

Anthropology is the scientific study of people, society, and culture. The writer gives a **definition** and an **example** of the new word.

A Read the following statements. Use context clues to identify the meanings of the words in bold. Then choose the correct definition.

1. Our devices also affect our mood. When they're lost, we **panic**. We're afraid we'll never see all the information we've recorded on our phones again.
   a. feel very calm   **b.** feel very frightened

2. For example, anyone can turn on a **webcam**, make a video of him- or herself, and post it on a video site.
   a. a video Web site   **b.** a camera connected to the Internet

3. Case believes that technology will continue to improve our lives. For example, she predicts that **mobile** devices of the future such as phones and tablets will analyze our daily activities. This will help us to do these activities in a more efficient way.
   a. easy to carry or move around   b. very heavy

4. Case hopes that technology of the future will **empower** us. She hopes that it will continue to extend our bodies and our minds, and make life better for everyone.
   a. cause problems   **b.** make stronger

B Scan Reading 2 for the following statements. Underline the phrases or statements in the context that help you understand the words in bold.

1. She believes our devices are turning us into **cyborgs** . . . (Par. 1)
2. Case calls herself a cyborg **anthropologist**. (Par. 1)
3. Your **digital self** is made up of . . . (Par. 3)
4. It also allows us to communicate easily with **networks** of people . . . (Par. 4)
5. They fulfill **specific** needs. (Par. 5)

C Compare answers to Exercise B with a partner. Work together to guess the meanings of the words in bold. Then decide whether the words and phrases you underlined are definitions, examples, or explanations.

Vocabulary Review

A Complete the paragraphs with the vocabulary below that you have studied in the unit.

be addicted to	done research on	on the whole	there is no question that
clearly illustrates	make the prediction	a perfect example	a valid concern

One of the most important uses of technology is to help keep us safe. This is especially true for technology associated with driving a car. _____ of this is a sensor that

1

provides the driver with a picture of what is behind the car. The sensor also makes a noise as you drive the car backward and the car gets close to something behind it. _____

2

these sensors can prevent accidents and save lives.

Experts have _____ the use of cell phones while driving that

3

_____ that this is a very dangerous habit. Yet many people appear to

4

_____ using their cell phones while driving. New technology may soon be

5

available to help them stop this dangerous behavior. This technology is in the cell phone itself. The technology responds to the movement of the car and prevents people from making calls while the car is moving. Even though most people know that the use of cell phones while driving is

_____ , most people do not like the idea of this technology.

6

_____ , however, people have already adapted to new laws about cell phone

7

use. Experts _____ that we will get used to this new technology, too.

8

B Compare answers to Exercise A with a partner. Then discuss the following questions.

Which car safety technology described in the reading do you think is a good idea? What other car safety technology would you invent?

Check surroundings for safety

C Complete the following sentences in a way that shows that you understand the meaning of the words in bold.

1. It's important for people **to have** something **in common** when _they get married_ .

2. My family is **made up of** _____ .

3. I believe you can **extend** your life if you _eat healthy_ _____

4. _____ is the most **efficient** way to _____ .

D Work with a partner and write four sentences that include any four of the vocabulary items below. You may use any verb tense and make nouns plural if you want.

contact information	interact with	readily available
have access to	to perform an operation on	similar interests

Connect the Readings

A Look back at Readings 1 and 2 to complete the chart below. Put a check (✓) in the boxes to show which topics appeared in each reading. Note that some topics appeared in both readings.

	Reading 1	Reading 2
1. Devices that feel like a part of your body		
2. Technology that lets you see information about things you are looking at		
3. Concerns about new technology		
4. Uses of cell phones		
5. Cell phone applications		
6. Technology that helps us to do things more efficiently		
7. Adapting to new technology		

B With a partner or in a small group, compare answers to Exercise A. Then discuss the following questions.

1. Find the topics that appear in both readings. In which reading was the topic more important?

2. Of all of the topics listed in Exercise A, which one was the most interesting to you? Explain why.

C Discuss the following questions with a partner. Use your understanding of the readings and your own ideas.

1. *Augmented reality* means improved reality. *Cyborgs* are improved humans. Do you agree that the technologies described in Readings 1 and 2 are improvements? Explain your answer.

2. Think about technology that would turn us into cyborgs. What technology do you think would be most useful to have as part of our bodies?

3. Describe a new technology you have recently heard about. How will it improve our lives?

MUSIC

A snake charmer, a kind of street performer, plays an instrument called a pungi in Thatta, Pakistan.

1. What types of music do you prefer? What types of music do you find unpleasant?

2. What are some benefits of listening to music? What are some benefits of playing a musical instrument?

Academic Vocabulary

challenging   invisible   physical
coordination   mental   visual

Handwritten annotations:
- It's / Asking / daring / arranged / working together to finish a common task
- something different / not able to be seen / material thing / in mind (related to your brain) / crazy / seen / being seen
- you can touch
- visual (vision)

Multiword Vocabulary

art form   in use
at one time   no doubt that
to be better at   to play a musical instrument

Handwritten annotations:
- type of art (music) / being use right now
- Same time / at one time (in the past) / it's sure / it's true
- do more / make Music

Reading Preview

A **Preview.** Read the title, the first paragraph, and the first and last sentence of each paragraph in Reading 1. The check (✓) four topics below that you think might be in this reading.

_____ 1. A comparison of music with other art forms

_____ 2. How a musician named Moby is helping scientists study the brain

_____ 3. The benefits of music

_____ 4. How scientists can see the effects of music on the brain

_____ 5. How music helps old people

_____ 6. How music helps people who have serious illnesses

B **Topic vocabulary.** The following words appear in Reading 1. Look at the words and answer the questions with a partner.

anxiety	hug	peers
elderly	memory	pleasurable
frightened	neuroscientists	reward

Handwritten annotations:
- 1 anxiety, 2 elderly, 1 frightened (afraid)
- 3 hug, 3 memory, neuroscientists
- Same age group; 1 peers, 1 pleasurable, reward 3

1. Which words make you think about good and bad feelings?

2. Which words relate to groups of people?

3. Which words make you think the reading might have something to do with the brain?

C **Predict.** What do you think this reading will be about? Discuss each word in Exercise B and predict how it may relate to the reading.

Handwritten margin note (vertical): Go to PowerPoint Practice / Math Lab

Music has the power to change the way we feel and even the way we behave. What else can music change? Read about some unexpected ways that music affects the brain.

The royal brass band play during festivities in Bhutan.

Seeing Music

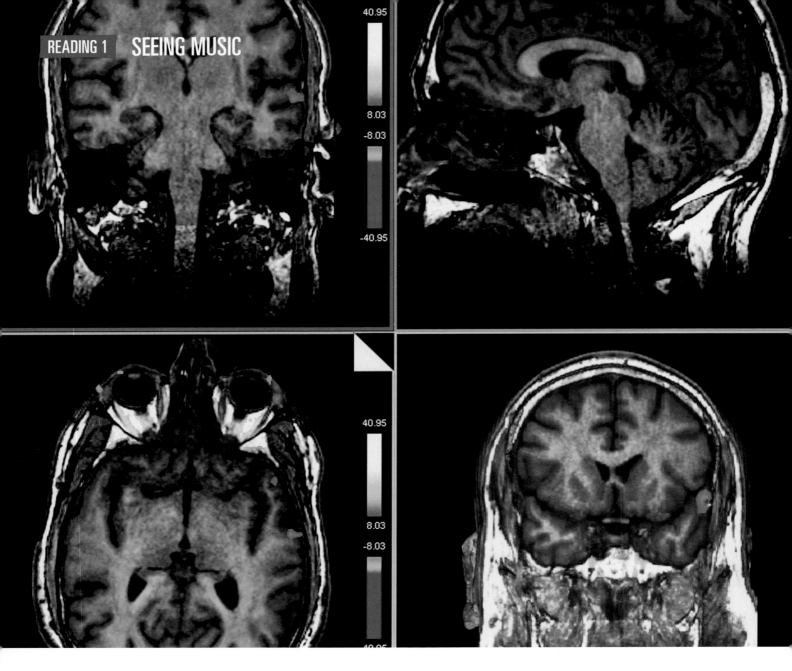

The musician Moby once said, "Music 1 has no form whatsoever—all it is is air moving just a little bit differently. It's the only art form that you can't touch." It is true that we cannot touch music, but that does not mean that music is an invisible art form. There is, in fact, a way to "see" music.

How can we see music? Neuroscientists, 2 people who study the human brain, use MRI machines (magnetic resonance imaging machines) to look inside the brain. These tools let them see what actually happens in the brain when people are doing things. For example, the tools let them see the neurons, or brain cells, that are in use when people are listening to music. Computer screens linked to MRIs show neurons lighting up when they are in use. And when people listen to music, neurons light up in many parts of the brain.

Neuroscientists have discovered that it isn't 3 necessary to hear music for the neurons to light up. Even when you just think about a song, these neurons light up. In addition, the same neural activity in the same part of the brain happens when people experience other pleasurable activities. For example, some of the same neurons light up when we eat something delicious or hug a loved one. This is because these neurons are in the areas of the brain that reward us by making us feel good. Negative feelings such as fear or anxiety make neurons in a different area light up. However, when an anxious or frightened person listens to pleasurable music, these neurons stop lighting up.

Now that neuroscientists can "see" the effects of music on the brain, they want to know what the benefits of music are. It turns out there are many benefits. Neuroscientists have discovered that music can help memory and may keep our brains young. Recent studies show that an elderly musician often has a better visual memory than an elderly non-musician. For example, elderly musicians are better at memorizing a written list of words than their non-musician peers.

Why does music have so many benefits? The answer may be because it uses so many different

> *"Now that neuroscientists can "see" the effects of music on the brain, they want to know what the benefits of music are."*

parts of the brain. According to neuroscientists, using many parts of the brain at one time gives your brain a good "workout."[1] In fact, one of the best brain "workouts" is to read music and play a musical instrument at the same time. Reading music while playing an instrument is a challenging task. It uses more parts of the brain simultaneously than most other activities and requires excellent coordination. It involves both physical movement and mental activity, much like playing a sport such as soccer.

So, although Moby is completely correct that we cannot touch music, it is possible to "see" the effect of music on our brains. There is still a lot to learn about the effects of music on our brains. However, there is no doubt that scientists have shown that music is an extremely powerful art form with many positive effects.

---

[1] *workout:* a period of physical or mental exercise or training

READING COMPREHENSION

Big Picture

Purpose (educate, teach, Give Knowledge
        Pursude, make you Laugh or Cry.

A Choose the answer that best completes each of the following sentences.

1. Paragraph 2 explains _____.
   a. how scientists "see" music
   b. what a brain cell is
   c. what a scientist does

2. The purpose of paragraph 3 is to explain _____.
   a. how music cures anxiety
   b. the brain's positive reaction to music
   c. why eating makes us feel good

3. The purpose of paragraph 4 is to _____.
   a. persuade people to study music
   b. show that music makes people smarter
   c. explore the benefits of music on the brain

4. The purpose of paragraph 5 is to _____.
   a. explain the difference between reading music and playing music
   b. compare listening to music to doing physical exercise
   c. explain why music has so many benefits

B Compare answers to Exercise A with a partner. Then reread the conclusion. The conclusion summarizes the main idea of the whole reading. With your partner, check (✓) the sentence below that best summarizes the reading. Discuss the reasons for your choice.

_____ **1.** Moby is correct that we cannot touch music.

_____ **2.** Neuroscience explains the benefits of music on our brains.

_____ **3.** We don't know everything about the effects of music yet.

_____ **4.** Music is extremely important.

Close-Up

A Decide which of the following statements are true or false according to the reading. Write *T* (True) or *F* (False) next to each one.

_____ **1.** Moby compares music to moving water.

_____ **2.** MRI machines allow researchers to see brain activity.

_____ **3.** When people listen to music, they use only one part of their brains.

_____ **4.** Thinking about a song does not produce the same brain activity as listening to a song.

_____ **5.** Anxiety and pleasurable music cause the same neurons to light up in the brain.

_____ **6.** Using different parts of our brain at the same time is good for us.

_____ **7.** According to the reading, older musicians often have better visual memories than older non-musicians.

_____ **8.** The reading compares playing music to playing a sport.

B Work with a partner or in a small group. Change the false statements in Exercise A to make them true.

Reading Skill

Taking Notes

Taking notes on a reading passage is a useful academic skill. Notes help you understand and remember what you've read. Taking notes can also help you to see the connections between main ideas and supporting ideas.

Here are a few tips for taking notes.

- You don't need to write complete sentences. You only need to write parts of sentences such as key words and phrases.
- You can abbreviate words; for example, you can use *ppl* for *people* and *comm.* for *communicate.*
- You can use common abbreviations such as *w/* for *with* and *e.g.* or *ex* for *for example.*
- You can use symbols such as arrows (→) and plus signs (+) to connect ideas.
- You can use ditto marks (") instead of repeating words.

A Read the following paragraph. Then follow the steps below to complete the notes in the outline.

Some doctors are using music to help patients with Alzheimer's disease. These are people who have _serious memory problems_ and _trouble communicating_. In addition, patients with Alzheimer's disease can become anxious and sometimes even get violent. Doctors who are using music to help patients with Alzheimer's disease have noticed several things. For one thing, they have found that music makes these patients less violent. It can also make them feel less stress or anxiety. Even more interesting, some doctors have found that patients with Alzheimer's disease who can't speak anymore can still sing. In addition, these patients can often remember the words to old songs.

- Underline the main idea of the paragraph.
- Complete the notes for the main idea in the outline below.
- Find the supporting ideas that explain the main idea.
- Complete the rest of the notes in the outline.

Main Idea: Some ~~Doctor~~ use music → help *Patient* w/Altz.

Supporting Ideas:
- Altz. patients have *Serius mem Proble* and *trouble com* ; + get *Anxious* & *Violen*
- music → *make these Pation less* violent
- " → less stress or *anxiety*
- Altz. patients can even *Sing*
- Altz. " can *often rem* song

B Use the outline below to take notes on paragraph 5 of Reading 1. Follow the steps in Exercise A.

Main Idea: *Why does music benefits*

Supporting Ideas:
- *Uses many te part of our brain*
- *Good workout*
- *Read music and Play*
- *exellent Coordination / Visical more and mental activities!*

C Compare your notes in Exercises A and B with a partner.

VOCABULARY PRACTICE

Academic Vocabulary

A Find the words in bold in Reading 1. Use the context to help you match each word to the correct definition.

_e_	**1. invisible** (Par. 1)	**a.**	of the mind
_c_	**2. visual** (Par. 4)	**b.**	hard
_b_	**3. challenging** (Par. 5)	**c.**	easy to see
_f_	**4. coordination** (Par. 5)	**d.**	of the body
_d_	**5. physical** (Par. 5)	**e.**	impossible to see
_a_	**6. mental** (Par. 5)	**f.**	skill

B Match the words on the left to the words on the right that they combine with in Reading 1.

_A_	**1. visual**	**a.**	art form
_e_	**2. challenging**	**b.**	memory
_D_	**3. excellent**	**c.**	activity
_F_	**4. physical**	**d.**	coordination
_B_	**5. invisible**	**e.**	task
_C_	**6. mental**	**f.**	movement

C Choose a phrase from Exercise B to complete each of the following sentences.

1. We can see paintings and sculptures, but music is different. It is a(n) _invisible art form_

2. Soccer requires _Excellen coord_ because you are running and trying to kick a ball at the same time.

3. Sara has a perfect _visual memory_. If she sees something once, she remembers it.

4. Learning to play the piano isn't easy. In fact, it can be a very _challeng task_ unless you practice it every day.

5. The _mental activities_ of doing crosswords and other puzzles is good for the brain.

6. Getting fit requires a lot of _physical movment_ as well as attention to diet.

Multiword Vocabulary

A Find the multiword vocabulary in bold in Reading 1. Then use the context and the sentences below to help you choose the correct definition.

1. Art students often study more than one **art form** (Par. 1) in college. For example, they may study both painting and sculpture.
   - **a.** type of art
   - **b.** work of art

2. At night, all the computers in the computer lab are **in use** (Par. 2).
   - **a.** being used
   - **b.** being repaired

3. Young children **are better at** (Par. 4) learning to pronounce foreign words than adults.
   - **a.** can do something very easily
   - **b.** can do something more easily than someone else

4. When it's noisy, it can be difficult to focus on more than one thing **at one time** (Par. 5).
   - **a.** at the same time
   - **b.** for one minute

5. Some music teachers use methods that teach children to **play a musical instrument** (Par. 5) without learning to read music.
   - **a.** listen to music
   - **b.** make music

6. There is **no doubt that** (Par. 6) sad music can make people feel sad.
   - **a.** it is not sure
   - **b.** it is sure

B Compare answers to Exercise A with a partner.

Use the Vocabulary

Write answers to the following questions. Use the words in bold in your answers. Then share your answers with a partner.

1. What subjects at school are or were particularly **challenging** for you?
2. Can you think of some sports that in your opinion, require **excellent coordination**? Name four.
3. What are some activities or games that require a great deal of **mental** focus?
4. What is your favorite kind of **visual art form**? Dancing
5. What things **are** you **better at** than most of your friends?
6. Do you **play a musical instrument**? If yes, which one(s)? If no, which musical instrument would you like to learn to play?

THINK AND DISCUSS

Work in a small group. Use the information in the reading and your own ideas to discuss the following questions.

1. **Apply knowledge.** According to what you learned in the reading, how do you think a psychologist could use music to help people who have emotional problems?

2. **Summarize.** What did you learn from the reading that would encourage you, if you were a parent, to have your children learn to play a musical instrument?

3. **Relate to personal experience.** Do different types of music ever affect the way you feel? Explain.

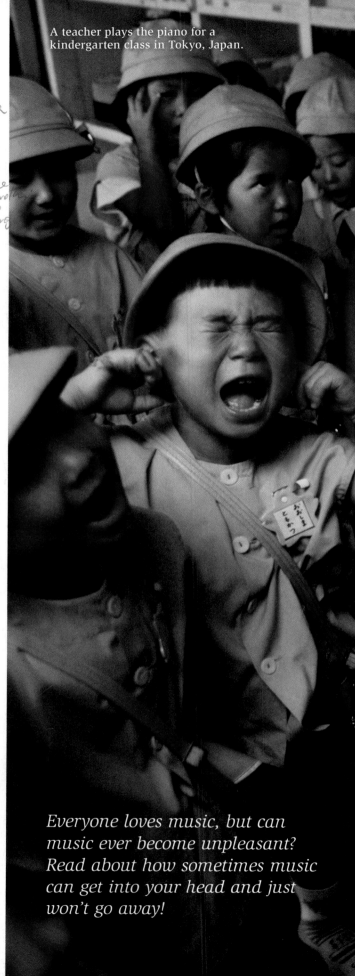

A teacher plays the piano for a kindergarten class in Tokyo, Japan.

Academic Vocabulary

[handwritten: usually natural]
[handwritten: unusual event]

to affect *(verb) (effect)*   a phenomenon   a strategy *[handwritten: A Plan]*

an incidence   to process   a theory *[handwritten: an idea]*

[handwritten: to change]
[handwritten: an event that happens once]
[handwritten: to think about]

Multiword Vocabulary

[handwritten: to not Forget]

to come in (first, second, etc.)   to stick in one's mind

to suffer from   *[handwritten: to be under the bad effect of something]*

it's no accident that   to take a test

over and over   *[handwritten: take a Short exam, or long quiz]*

[handwritten: to win a competition, It happened on Purpose, many]

Reading Preview

A Preview. Read the title of Reading 2. Look at the photos and Figure 1 on pages 94–97 and read their captions. Then discuss the following questions with a partner or in a small group.

1. What do you think an *earworm* is?

2. What part of the body is Reading 2 about?

3. What part of the brain is connected to hearing?

4. What kind of a scientist is Dr. Sacks?

B Topic vocabulary. The following words appear in Reading 2. Look at the words and answer the questions with a partner.

2 advertisements   repetitiveness *3*   sound *2*

1 annoying   research *3*   suffered *1*

1 irritate   song *2*   surveyed *3*

[handwritten: Asking question]

1. Which words have to do with something unpleasant?

2. Which words relate to things you might hear?

3. Which words make you think the reading will include a scientific study?

C Predict. What do you think this reading will be about? Discuss each word in Exercise B and predict how it may relate to the reading.

Everyone loves music, but can music ever become unpleasant? Read about how sometimes music can get into your head and just won't go away!

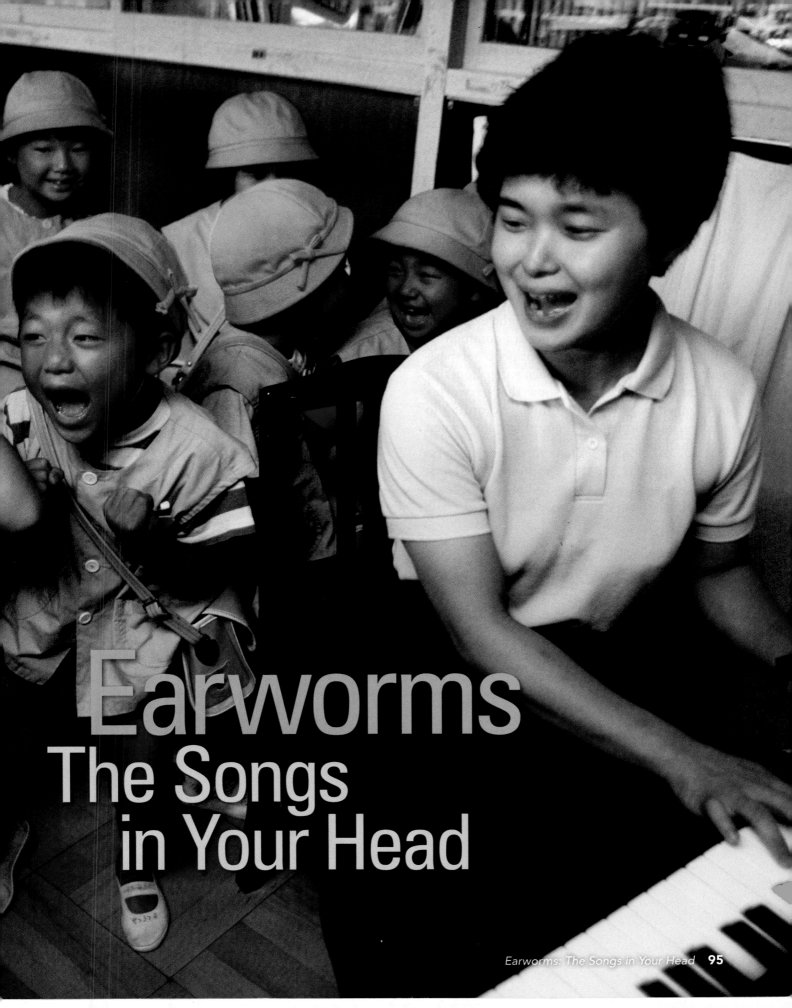

Earworms
The Songs
in Your Head

Close-Up

A Choose the best answer for each of the following questions.

1. What percentage of people experience earworms?
   a. 60 percent
   b. 90 percent

2. Who is more irritated by earworms?
   a. women
   b. men

3. Who thinks earworms may be a result of all the music in our environment?
   a. Oliver Sacks
   b. James Kellaris

4. What kind of information does the auditory cortex process?
   a. things you see
   b. things you hear

5. Who believes there are three characteristics of a song that will become an earworm?
   a. Oliver Sacks
   b. James Kellaris

6. What is "Dr. Earworm's" job?
   a. He's a medical doctor.
   b. He's a college professor.

7. Which sentence best describes an earworm song?
   a. It keeps repeating the same tune or words.
   b. It is a song that is used in advertising.

8. Who did Kellaris ask to participate in the study?
   a. college students
   b. advertisers

9. According to the research, which jingle became an earworm for more people?
   a. the candy bar jingle
   b. the restaurant jingle

10. What is a tip for getting rid of an earworm?
    a. sing the earworm over and over again
    b. distract yourself with an activity

B Compare answers to Exercise A with a partner. If you don't agree, find statements in Reading 2 that support your answers.

Reading Skill

Identifying Pronoun References

Pronouns usually refer to nouns or noun phrases that appear earlier in a text. The pronoun may refer to a noun earlier in the sentence or in a previous sentence. It's important to understand which noun a pronoun refers to.

Subject pronouns include *I*, *he*, *she*, *it*, *you*, *we*, and *they*.

Object pronouns include *me*, *him*, *her*, *it*, *you*, *us*, and *them*.

Pronouns match the noun they refer to in gender and in number.

> **An earworm song** is usually simple, and **it** usually has words, too.
> singular neutral   singular neutral
> noun   subject pronoun

> **Kellaris** is a professor, and **he** also plays music.
> singular male   singular male
> noun   subject pronoun

He refers to Kellaris
Kellaris is the referant of it

NB

> *After the professor tested the **woman**, he asked **her** to rank the songs.*
> singular female   singular female
> noun   object pronoun
>
> *When you hear **jingles**, you often remember **them**.*
> plural neutral   plural neutral
> noun   object pronoun

A Find the following sentences in Reading 2. Write the word or words that each underlined pronoun refers to.

1. Paragraph 1: You keep hearing it, over and over again.
   Song

2. Paragraph 2: What are earworms, and why do we get them?
   ears worms

3. Paragraph 2: A study showed that 90 percent of people experience them.
   ear worm

4. Paragraph 4: It's a short-term storage system for small amounts of auditory (sound) information.
   auditory cortex

5. Paragraph 4: Some of this auditory information is forgotten, and some of it goes into long-term memory.
   auditory Information

6. Paragraph 5: He thinks that only certain types of songs become earworms.
   James

7. Paragraph 6: They are an important part of selling products.
   Jingles.

8. Paragraph 6: Advertisers want jingles to stick in people's minds to keep them thinking about their products.
   People's mind

B Compare answers to Exercise A with a partner.

VOCABULARY PRACTICE

Academic Vocabulary

A Find the words in bold in Reading 2. Use the context to help you match each word to the correct definition.

_A_	**1. phenomenon** (Par. 2)	**a.** something that happens or exists in the world
_E_	**2. theories** (Par. 3)	**b.** deals with (information, products, etc.) in a systematic way
_d_	**3. affects** (Par. 3)	**c.** plans you use to achieve something
_F_	**4. incidence** (Par. 3)	**d.** has an influence on a person or a thing
_C_	**5. processes** (Par. 4)	**e.** ideas that try to explain something
_B_	**6. strategies** (Par. 7)	**f.** the occurrence of something at a particular time

B Choose the correct word in the box below to complete each of the following sentences. Notice and learn the words in bold because they often appear with the academic words.

affects	incidence	phenomenon	processes	strategies	theories

1. A song with a regular beat often **greatly** _affects_ my mood. It can make me feel happy and energetic.

2. A computer _process_ **information** in a way that is similar to the brain.

3. The researcher noticed **a high** _incidence_ **of** earworms in mall shoppers. A large number of people could not forget the songs they heard while they were shopping at a mall.

4. A neuroscience team **tested** several _theories_ about earworms by doing a research study.

5. Some people have ESP—extrasensory perception. For example, they know who is ringing the doorbell before they open the door. ESP is **an unexplained** _phenomenon_ because scientists still don't understand it.

6. **Effective** _strategies_ for memorizing a new song include singing it over and over again.

Multiword Vocabulary

A Find the multiword vocabulary in bold in Reading 2. Use the context to help you complete each definition.

1. If something happens **over and over** (Par. 1), it happens _____.
   a. one time
   b. a lot

2. If you are **taking a test** (Par. 1), you are probably _____.
   a. teaching someone how to do something
   b. showing a teacher what you have learned

3. If you **suffer from** (Par. 2) a condition, you _a_ .
   a. have it
   b. no longer have it

4. When you say **it's no accident that** (Par. 6) something exists, _____.
   a. it seems logical
   b. it seems unusual

5. When things **stick in people's minds** (Par. 6), people _____.
   a. forget them
   b. remember them

6. If something **came in second** (Par. 6) in a survey, it was _____.
   a. at the top
   b. not at the top

B Complete the following sentences with the correct multiword vocabulary from Exercise A. Use the words in parentheses to help you.

1. Students learn new vocabulary when they hear words and phrases ___over and over___ (many times).

2. Advertising jingles are hard to forget. The advertisers who write the jingles want them to ___stick in your mind___ (be easy to remember for a long time).

3. If you are ___taking a test___ (answering a set of questions) in the morning, it's not a good idea to stay up all night studying.

4. ___It's no accident___ (It's not by chance that) jingles become earworms. Jingle writers write them with all the characteristics of earworms.

5. If you ___suffer from___ (have a problem with) memory problems, it's a good idea to do crosswords and other games that exercise your brain.

6. In a survey of popular songs and jingles, "Like a Rolling Stone" was first on the list and "Imagine" ___came in second___ (appeared directly after).

Use the Vocabulary

Write answers to the following questions. Use the words in bold in your answers. Then share your answers with a partner.

1. What are some **strategies** that you use when you are going to **take a test**?

2. Is there an unexplained **phenomenon** that fascinates you, for example, UFOs (unidentified flying objects) or ESP? ___People Think Something And you know it___

3. Do you **process** some types of information more quickly and easily than other types? Explain your answer.

4. Have you ever **come in first** or **second** in a competition or a contest? If yes, describe it.

5. Do the words of any poems **stick in your mind**? Which ones?

6. How does a song **affect** you when you hear it **over and over** again? Do you get an earworm?

THINK AND DISCUSS

Work in a small group. Use the information in the reading and your own ideas to discuss the following questions.

1. **Relate to personal experience.** Think of an advertising jingle or popular song that became an earworm for you. What was it?

2. **Summarizing and evaluating.** According to the reading, what are the solutions to the problem of earworms? Which ones do you think would work for you?

3. **Evaluate the author's opinion.** The author believes that earworms are always annoying. Does the author support this belief? If so, how? Do you agree? Why, or why not?

Vocabulary Review

Ⓐ Complete the paragraphs with the vocabulary below that you have studied in the unit.

came in second	an effective strategy	processes information	take a test
challenging task	no doubt that	stick in your mind	tested this theory

   Neuroscientists have thought for a long time that listening to music can improve memory, and

researchers at Missouri Western State College recently _____. The researchers

1

were interested in whether different types of sounds affect how the brain

_____, so they had three groups of volunteers _____.

2   3

One group listened to classical music while they looked at a picture. Another listened to rock

music. The third group listened to a sort of noise—not music at all. They then answered questions

about the picture. The classical music group did the best, and the rock group

_____; the group that listened to just noise did not do well.

4

   This research is good news for college students. Many students find it a stressful and

_____ when they have to memorize information for a test. Now they know

5

that _____ for improving memory may involve listening to music while they

6

study. You don't have to like classical music, either, because there seems to be

_____ listening to any kind of music while studying can make it easier to get

7

new information to _____.

8

B Compare answers to Exercise A with a partner. Then discuss the following questions.

Are you surprised by the test results in the experiment? Why, or why not?

C Complete the following sentences in a way that shows that you understand the meaning of the words in bold.

1. My favorite **art form** is _____.

2. I **am better at** _____ than I am at _____.

3. An example of **visual memory** is when you _____.

4. The best form of **mental activity** is _____.

D Work with a partner and write four sentences that include any four of the vocabulary items below. You may use any verb tense and make any nouns plural if you want.

excellent coordination	physical movement	suffer from
over and over	play a musical instrument	unexplained phenomenon

Connect the Readings

A Look back at Readings 1 and 2 to answer the questions in the chart below. Work with a partner and check (✓) the correct boxes for each answer.

	Reading 1	Reading 2
1. Which reading talks more about brain research?		
2. Which reading discusses the value of music in learning?		
3. Which reading talks about using music to sell products?		
4. Which reading contains research on older people?		
5. Which reading contains research on male and female differences?		
6. Which reading compares playing music to a form of exercise?		
7. Which reading includes strategies for dealing with a problem?		

B With a partner or in a small group, compare answers to Exercise A. Then discuss the following questions.

1. Which reading had more valuable information for you? Why?

2. What did you learn about music and the brain that you didn't already know?

C Discuss the following questions with a partner. Use your understanding of the readings and your own ideas.

1. What does brain research tell us about music and the brain? What else would you like to know about music and the brain?

2. What are some of the benefits of listening to music?

3. What is one disadvantage to listening to music?

A herd of red lechwes runs across
flooded grasslands in Botswana.

Animal Groups

FOCUS

1. What wild animals live in large groups?

2. What are the advantages for animals of living in large groups?

READING 1

Why do some animals live together in large groups while others live alone? Learn about different types of animal "families"—from birds to monkeys.

Academic Vocabulary ~~very important~~ ~~strongest~~

to work together

to cooperate   dominant   to protect

to determine   dramatic   status *Position*

to focus on, to decide ~~emotional~~ ~~very strong~~ *Level of importance*

Multiword Vocabulary *Big change* *better Protection*

Every once a while, not often

from time to time   safety in numbers *you Stronger with other around yo*

to not fight with

to get along with   to take over *take command, Control of*

to keep watch over   when it comes to *Speaking about something*

to Look care fully

to guard   *when it happens.*

Reading Preview

A **Preview.** Quickly read the subheadings and small fact boxes and look at the photos on pages 108–111. Then discuss the following questions with a partner or in a small group.

1. What animal groups are included in the reading?

2. What kinds of information about the animal groups are in the reading?

3. What are some differences among the animal groups?

B **Topic vocabulary.** The following words appear in Reading 1. Look at the words and answer the questions with a partner.

make babies

(hyena) 2 breed   2 hunt   3 offspring *(babies)*

1 clans   3 leader   1 packs *(Wolves)*

(bees/Flam) 1 colony   2 mate   1 troop *(Langurs)*

(ings) follower   *get in group of two*

1. Which words describe groups of animals?

2. Which words relate to things that animals do?

3. Which words describe roles or relationships among animals in groups?

C **Predict.** What do you think this reading will be about? Discuss each word in Exercise B and predict how it may relate to the reading.

American Flamingoes and their young in Yucatan, Mexico

Living Together

M any animal species live together in groups. Some of these groups 1 are very large, with over a million individuals. Other animals live in smaller family groups. There's often one leader and many followers. Animals that live in groups range from birds to wolves to monkeys, and group behavior can include hunting, eating, and raising their offspring together.

Chilean Flamingoes

These famous pink birds live in very large 2 groups called colonies. A typical colony consists of several dozen birds, but amazingly, some groups have a million or more individuals. Flamingoes eat, fly, and breed together. To eat, they bury their bills, or even their entire heads, in the mud beneath shallow water. While they are completely unprotected when they are eating, there is safety in numbers. Living in large groups helps to protect them from predators[1] while their heads are down in the mud. Some flamingoes keep watch over the colony while the other members eat.

Type: Bird
Group Name: Colony
Location: South America
Diet: Small marine organisms such as plankton and tiny fish

Flamingoes also have unusual breeding 3 and parenting habits. When flamingoes breed, both parents sit on the nest until their eggs hatch. Baby flamingoes then join a "nursery." Adults take turns looking after the babies in the nursery while other parents fly off to get food. Some nurseries have over 30,000 babies. Even in this big crowd, parent flamingoes can always find their own offspring when they return from hunting for food.

---
[1] *predators:* animals that kill and eat other animals

Gray Wolves

Wolves are sociable animals and do almost everything together. They live in family groups of 6 to 15 but, from time to time, unrelated adult males join the pack, too. Wolf packs have a hierarchy[1] of leadership. In this hierarchy, one male leads the pack with his mate close by. This is the only pair in the pack that can have offspring. The male leader and his mate are the oldest members and the best hunters of the pack. They make all the decisions for the pack. For example, they decide where to go and when to hunt. The rest of the pack consists of young adults and pups.[2] The young adults have their own hierarchy, but they must follow the lead of the male leader. The lowest members of the hierarchy are the wolf pups. However, even the pups challenge each other and play at being the boss. This practice helps determine whether a pup will be a leader one day. All the older members of the pack help to raise the pups. They protect the pups and bring them food.

4

Type: Mammal
Group Name: Pack
Location: North America, parts of Europe, Russia, and China
Diet: Meat

[1] *hierarchy:* a system of organizing people, animals, or things into different levels of importance

[2] *pups:* baby animals, especially from the dog family

Spotted Hyenas

Spotted hyenas live together in large groups 5 called clans. These groups may include up to 80 individuals. Female hyenas have a dominant role in the group. Female hyenas are larger than the males, and they are the leaders of the clan. Even the females with the lowest rank[1] in a clan have power over male hyenas. While wolves often cooperate with one another, hyenas are somewhat competitive.[2] Hyena clans hunt together, but they fight over their food. They chase and kill their prey together, but then they compete with each other to eat the most. This means hyenas are speed eaters. One hyena can eat a gazelle, a small African deer, in less than two minutes. When it comes to raising the young, females only look after their own children, and males don't help out at all.

Type: Mammal
Group Name: Clan
Location: Africa
Diet: Plants and meat

---

[1] *rank:* position in a group or hierarchy

[2] *competitive:* trying to be more successful than the others in a group

Tufted Gray Langurs

Gray langurs live in groups of 11 to 60 individuals. There are three types of gray langur groups: groups with one male and several females and their offspring; groups with several males, females, and children; and all-male groups. Male langurs lead all three types of groups. The male becomes a leader after fighting for that position. The males tend to be very aggressive[1] with each other. Although females aren't leaders of the complete group, they also have their own hierarchy. Physical condition—not fighting—determines female hierarchy. This means that the youngest

_____
[1] *aggressive:* behaving angrily or violently toward others

6

Type: Mammal
Group Name: Troop
Location: India and Sri Lanka
Diet: Fruit and insects

females usually have the highest status because they are the fittest and healthiest. Female langurs usually get along with each other.

7

Only the highest-ranking males in a mixed group may breed. These high-ranking individuals can mate with any female in the group. Langur groups can go through dramatic changes. For example, a new male from another group sometimes challenges the male leader and takes over the group. As part of the attack, the new male kills all the offspring of the former leader.

READING COMPREHENSION

Big Picture

A Read the following pairs of sentences for each section of Reading 1. In each pair, write *MI* next to the main idea and *SD* next to the supporting detail.

1. Chilean Flamingoes

SD _____ **a.** Flamingoes help each other look after their babies.

MI _____ **b.** Flamingoes live in very large groups in order to protect each other.

2. Gray Wolves

SD _____ **a.** The leaders of the wolf pack make all the decisions for the group.

MI _____ **b.** Wolves live together in groups and do many things together.

3. Spotted Hyenas

MI _____ **a.** Spotted hyenas live in large groups headed by females.

SD _____ **b.** Hyenas eat very quickly.

4. Tufted Gray Langurs

SD _____ **a.** Male langurs kill babies in order to become the new leader.

MI _____ **b.** Gray langurs live together in three types of groups called troops.

B Compare answers to Exercise A with a partner.

Close-Up

A Decide which of the following statements are true or false according to the reading. Write *T* (True) or *F* (False) next to each one.

F _____ **1.** Flamingoes live in groups of at least a dozen members.

T _____ **2.** Flamingoes are in danger when they eat.

F _____ **3.** Flamingo groups are so large that parents can never find their offspring.

T _____ **4.** Wolf packs can include individuals that are not related to each other.

F _____ **5.** A wolf pack consists of several adult males.

F _____ **6.** Low-ranking male hyenas have power over low-ranking female hyenas.

F _____ **7.** Hyenas don't hunt together.

F _____ **8.** Females are the leaders in langur troops.

F _____ **9.** High-ranking female langurs are the best fighters.

T _____ **10.** Low-ranking langur males in mixed troops cannot breed.

B Work with a partner or in a small group. Change the false statements in Exercise A to make them true.

C Scan the fact boxes in Reading 1 to answer the following questions.

1. Which animals are mammals? _hyenas, Langurs, Wolves_
2. Which animal lives in Africa? _hyenas_
3. Which animals eat only meat? _Wolves._

Reading Skill

Organizing Information in a Chart

When you organize information in a chart, it helps you to understand the ideas in the reading. It also helps you to recognize relationships among the ideas, such as similarities and differences.

A Complete the chart below with information from Reading 1. If there is no information in the reading for an item in the chart, write *no information*. One answer for each category is done for you.

Animal	Size of Group	Who Raises the Offspring	Group Leader	Process to Choose Leader
Chilean Flamingoes	dozen or million	Parents and other adults	nada	no information
Gray Wolves	6 to 15	all the other adults	one male	
Spotted Hyenas	up to 80	only females	only Female	strongest
Tufted Gray Langurs	11–60 individuals	nada	males	fighting kill babies of old teeth

B Use the chart in Exercise A to write short answers to the following questions.

1. Which animal group can have the most members? _flama_
2. Which animal group can have the fewest members? _Wolves_
3. In which animal groups do both males and females take care of the young? _Flaming wolves_
4. In which animal group is a female the group leader? _hyena_
5. In which group does the winner of a fight get selected as leader? _Langur_

VOCABULARY PRACTICE

Academic Vocabulary

A Find the words in bold in Reading 1. Use the context to help you match sentence parts to create definitions.

_d_ **1.** To **protect** (Par. 2) someone

_e_ **2.** To **determine** (Par. 4) something

_c_ **3.** If something is **dominant** (Par. 5),

_f_ **4.** To **cooperate** (Par. 5)

_b_ **5.** An individual's **status** (Par. 6)

_a_ **6.** If something is **dramatic** (Par. 7),

a. it is sudden or surprising.

b. is his or her position in a group.

c. it is more powerful, successful, or noticeable than other things.

d. is to keep someone safe.

e. is to make a decision about it.

f. is to work together or help each other.

B Read the following sentences and choose the correct word to complete each one. The correct word often appears with the academic word in bold.

1. Certain factors **determine** _____ a new male will become the leader in a chimpanzee group.
   a. which   **b.** whether

2. Penguins often swim in large groups. This helps **protect** them _____ predators.
   a. from   **b.** to

3. When the leader of a wolf pack dies, there are often **dramatic** _____ in the group. There can be a lot of fighting until a new leader emerges.
   a. changes   **b.** forces

4. Even weaker female hyenas have a **dominant** _____ over male hyenas. One reason may be because female hyenas are larger than males.
   a. top   **b.** role

5. Trina, a young female gorilla, **cooperates** _____ the zookeepers.
   a. to   **b.** with

6. Unrelated adult wolves don't have _____ **status** in their packs. Even though they are old, they don't have any power.
   a. high   **b.** strong

Multiword Vocabulary

A Find the words in the box below in Reading 1. Then use the words from the box to complete the multiword vocabulary.

along	comes to	in numbers	keep	over	time

1. safety _in numbers_ (Par. 2)

2. _keep_ _____ **watch over** (Par. 2)

3. from _time_ **to time** (Par. 4)

4. when it _comes to_ (Par. 5)

5. get _along_ **with** (Par. 6)

6. takes _over_ (Par. 7)

B Complete the following sentences with the correct multiword vocabulary from Exercise A.

1. Some animals do not feel protected unless they live in large groups. They find _Safety in_____. Zebras are a good example of this.

2. It is unusual for males in many animal groups to ___*Keep watch*_____ their young. It is usually the females who take care of their offspring.

3. _When it's co_____ removing the leader of a troop, gray langurs can be very aggressive.

4. Most wolf packs do not have any unrelated adult males, but _From time to_____ an unrelated adult male is accepted into a group.

5. Once a new wolf _____*takes over*_____ the group, he has the dominant role and is the only male that can breed.

6. Young wolves sometimes don't ___*Get along with*_____ their brothers and sisters very well when they are young. They often fight.

Use the Vocabulary

Write answers to the following questions. Use the words in bold in your answers. Then share your answers with a partner.

1. Which professions in your community have the highest **status**? Why do they have high **status**?

2. Do you like to **cooperate** with other students on group projects? Or do you prefer to work alone? Give examples.

3. How do you feel when a **dominant** individual in a group **takes over**? Does it bother you? Why, or why not?

4. Do you **take over** group situations **from time to time**? Why, or why not?

5. Is there anyone you don't **get along with**? Explain your answer.

6. How do you **determine** which classes you will take each term? What factors do you consider?

THINK AND DISCUSS

Work in a small group. Use the information in the reading and your own ideas to discuss the following questions.

1. **Summarize.** What did you learn about the behavior of animals in groups? Did any information surprise you? Explain.

2. **Identify similarities.** How is animal behavior in groups similar to human behavior in groups?

3. **Express an opinion.** Is it useful to study animal behavior? What can we learn from animal behavior?

Academic Vocabulary

a conflict   intelligent   a location
furthermore   an interaction   suitable

Handwritten annotations:
A fight — argument — smart — place
So, also, moreover — meeting betw 2 ppl — good enough / good match

Multiword Vocabulary

to be in charge   in search of
close together   a key component
to follow the rules   to solve a problem

Handwritten annotations:
be the boss
near, not far, not touching
to do what
2 people
Looking for something.
an import part
have a solution
to an issue

A school of sardines appear like a tornado, Pescador Island, Philippines.

Reading Preview

A **Preview.** Read the title of Reading 1 and the first paragraph on page 118. Look at the photos on pages 116–118 and read their captions. Make a list of three questions you think this reading might answer. Use *which, why, what, how, how many,* or *when.* Then discuss your questions with a partner or in a small group.

1. _____
2. _____
3. _____

B **Topic vocabulary.** The following words appear in Reading 2. Look at the words and answer the questions with a partner.

architects *(1)*   queen *(1)*   staff *(1)*
hive *(3)*   scout *(1)*   survival *(2)*
managers *(1)*   soldiers   threats *(2)*
nests *(3)*

1. Which words describe roles or jobs?
2. Which words relate to danger?
3. Which words are places animals live?

C **Predict.** What do you think this reading will be about? Discuss each word in Exercise B and predict how it may relate to the reading.

Enter the world of swarms and discover how some insects and animals can accomplish amazing things when they work together.

The Genius of
SWARMS

A swarm of wood ants work together to move a leaf.

1   What do ants, bees, pigeons, and herrings have in common? All these animals swarm. Swarming occurs when large numbers of individual animals move, work, or cooperate as a group. Swarming animals can act quickly to solve a problem. They can respond effectively to threats. Swarms appear to know exactly where they are going, what they are doing, and why they are doing it. Scientific research is helping us understand how swarming works so well.

2   Ants are a good example of swarming animals. Swarms of ants can do many difficult tasks. For example, they can find the shortest path to the best food source. It may appear that individual ants build nests and defend their homes, but ants aren't clever architects or soldiers—at least not as individuals. When it comes to deciding what to do next, most ants seem lost on their own. According to Deborah M. Gordon, a biologist at Stanford University, "If you watch an ant try to accomplish something, you'll be impressed by how inept[1] it is." Although individual ants don't appear to be very intelligent, as colonies they are intelligent. This is because they use swarm intelligence.

3   Swarm intelligence is the collective[2] behavior of large groups. The key feature of swarm intelligence seems to be that no one is in charge. In

---

[1] *inept:* completely lacking skill
[2] *collective:* involving every member of the group

the case of ants, there appear to be no leaders. No ant seems to be telling any other ants what to do. There is a queen ant, but her only role is to lay eggs. Yet, a colony of half a million ants functions perfectly without any managers at all. Furthermore, no single ant seems to have any knowledge about the big picture—the main goals or objectives. The swarm relies on lots of interaction between individuals who all follow the rules. One of these rules is to stay close together. When individuals stay close together, they communicate and share a lot of information.

Different animals have different methods of interaction. For example, ants leave a trail of pheromones[3] for other ants to follow. A key component of bee interaction is movement. When bees need to move their hive to a new place, scout bees go out in search of a suitable place to live. When they return, they each do a type of dance. The "happier" the bee is about the new location, the faster the dance is. In addition, the dance includes a code with directions to the new location. The excited dancers excite other scout bees. These bees then fly out to check out the new locations. They come back, get close together, and dance with the other excited bees. The bees will not move until they are all "excited," or in agreement about the best location. Once a large enough group of bees all agree, they convince the thousands of other bees. Then they all fly together to the new location.

> " The swarm relies on lots of interaction between individuals who all follow the rules. "

4

Scientists are realizing how effective swarm 5 intelligence is. Some scientists are applying what they've learned to solve human problems.

Thomas Seeley, a biologist at Cornell University, is impressed by how well bees make decisions. So, he uses swarm intelligence in his meetings. Seeley doesn't tell his staff what to do or make all the decisions. Instead, he asks his staff to identify all the possibilities, discuss their ideas, and then vote by ballot.[4] Seeley wants his staff, like the bees, to focus on the group's needs, not on the individual ideas. "It . . . gives a group time to let the best ideas emerge and win." Seeley says that running meetings using swarm intelligence ideas can lead to better decisions. It can also reduce conflict among the staff.

In nature, animals use swarm intelligence for 6 survival. Large numbers increase their chances of finding food, following a migration route, or avoiding predators. For these animals, working together is a matter of life or death. For humans, there is much to learn from swarm intelligence to make our lives more efficient.

---

[3] *pheromones:* chemicals that some insects and animals produce. Pheromones can affect the behavior of other animals and insects of the same type.

---

[4] *ballot:* a secret vote

READING COMPREHENSION

Big Picture

(A) Answer the following questions about the paragraphs in Reading 2. Write the correct paragraph number on the line.

___3___ **1.** In which paragraph does the author define *swarm intelligence*?

___5___ **2.** In which paragraph does the author give examples of how swarm intelligence can help humans?

___4___ **3.** In which paragraph does the author describe the behavior of bees?

___2___ **4.** In which paragraph does the author give an example of a swarming animal?

B Read the following statements. Check (✓) the one that expresses the author's purpose for writing Reading 2.

_____ **1.** To describe the intelligence of ants

___✗___ **2.** To show what we can learn from swarm intelligence

_____ **3.** To show how ants and bees are similar

Close-Up

A Choose the answer that best completes each of the following sentences.

1. Ants, bees, pigeons, and herrings _____.
   a. are the smartest swarming animals
   b. are examples of swarming animals
   c. behave the same way as humans

2. One of the characteristics of swarm intelligence is _____.
   a. that there are no leaders
   b. that individuals don't work together as a group
   c. that individuals understand the big picture

3. Individual ants _____.
   a. interact using pheromones
   b. are intelligent
   c. don't have roles

4. Bees communicate _____.
   a. by dancing
   b. by touching each other
   c. by making more noise

5. Thomas Seeley thinks that swarm intelligence can help humans _____.
   a. improve their intelligence
   b. improve their decision making
   c. increase conflict

B Compare answers to Exercise A with a partner. Then answer the questions you wrote for Exercise A on page 116.

Reading Skill

Recognizing Facts and Theories

Good readers notice the difference between facts and theories presented in a reading. In academic writing, authors use facts to support their main ideas or to report on the ideas of others. Authors also include theories or ideas that they believe are true, but that they are not yet certain about. When they aren't certain about something, they use words like _seem_, _appear_, and _suggest_.

Fact: _Swarming occurs when large numbers of individual animals move, work, or cooperate as a group._

Theory: _Swarms appear to know exactly where they are going, what they are doing, and why they are doing it._

A Read the following paragraph. Decide if the sentences are presented as facts or theories. Then write *Fact* or *Theory* on the lines below.

How does an ant colony decide what to do without a leader? (1) Ants communicate by touch and smell. (2) When one ant bumps into another, they sniff each other with their antennae. (3) The ants seem to be sniffing to find out if the other ant belongs to the same nest or not. (4) The ants also appear to be using their antennae to figure out where the other ants have been working. (5) Ants that work outside the nest smell different from those that stay inside. (6) In addition, every morning, some ants go out and return to the nest before the others leave. (7) As the first group enters the nest, the ants touch antennae briefly with the ants about to go out. (8) This suggests that some ants wait for the other ants to find a food source for them. (9) After the others return, it appears that they use their antennae to discover where the first group of ants found the food source.

1. _fact_   4. _T_   7. _F_

2. _F_   5. _F_   8. _T_

3. _T_   6. _F_   9. _T_

B Reread paragraph 1 in Reading 2. Find the one theory and write it below.

Theory: _Swarms appear to know Exactly_

C Read the following statements from paragraph 2 in Reading 2. Write *Fact* or *Theory* next to each one.

Fact   **1.** Swarms of ants can do many difficult tasks.

_F_   **2.** For example, they can find the shortest path to the best food source.

Theo   **3.** It may appear that individual ants build nests and defend their homes, . . .

_F_   **4.** . . . but ants aren't clever architects or soldiers—at least not as individuals.

D Read the following sentences from paragraph 3 in Reading 2. Write *Fact* or *Theory* on the lines before each sentence.

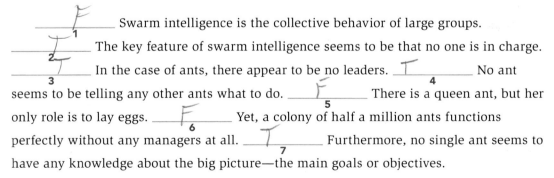

_F_ Swarm intelligence is the collective behavior of large groups.

_T_ The key feature of swarm intelligence seems to be that no one is in charge.

_T_ In the case of ants, there appear to be no leaders. _T_ No ant seems to be telling any other ants what to do. _F_ There is a queen ant, but her only role is to lay eggs. _F_ Yet, a colony of half a million ants functions perfectly without any managers at all. _T_ Furthermore, no single ant seems to have any knowledge about the big picture—the main goals or objectives.

VOCABULARY PRACTICE

Academic Vocabulary

A Find the words in bold in Reading 2. Use the context to help you choose the definition that is closest to the meaning in the paragraph.

1. **intelligent** (Par. 2)   **a.** fast   **b.** smart
2. **furthermore** (Par. 3)   **a.** additionally   **b.** besides
3. **interaction** (Par. 3)   **a.** relations   **b.** contact
4. **suitable** (Par. 4)   **a.** right   **b.** appropriate
5. **location** (Par. 4)   **a.** place   **b.** exact position
6. **conflict** (Par. 5)   **a.** struggle   **b.** war

B Choose an academic word from Exercise A to complete each of the following sentences. Notice and learn the words in bold because they often appear with the academic words.

1. Although individual animals in a swarm may not seem **very** _____, the swarm itself can do quite complicated tasks.

2. Most pigeons build their nests in a variety of locations. It doesn't take them long to find a(n) _____ **place**.

3. When pigeons fly as a group, they use swarm intelligence. The _____ **between** the birds ensures that they rarely crash into each other.

4. The restaurant was never busy, so the owners decided to move it to a **new** _____ closer to the center of the city.

5. Some people think that using swarm intelligence to make decisions will **reduce** _____. This is because no one individual makes the decisions.

Multiword Vocabulary

A Find the multiword vocabulary in bold in Reading 2. Use the context to help you understand the meaning. Then match the multiword vocabulary in each sentence to its correct definition.

1. Many organizations are using the Internet to get large numbers of people to exchange ideas in order to **solve a problem** (Par. 1). This is called "crowdsourcing."
   a. find an answer   **b.** ignore information

2. Human groups, especially groups of children, usually work better together when someone **is in charge** (Par. 3).
   a. has the role of leader   **b.** leaves them alone

3. If all the people in a community **follow the rules** (Par. 3), their lives will be more pleasant and peaceful.
   a. do what an individual thinks is right   **b.** do what a group has decided is right

4. Many people feel uncomfortable when they have to move in tightly packed groups. On the other hand, many insects stay very **close together** (Par. 3) in order to survive.
   a. near to each other   **b.** far from each other

5. **A key component** (Par. 4) of group decision making is discussing all of the possible results of the decision with the group members.

   a. one of the steps **b.** an important part

6. When bees go **in search of** (Par. 4) a new home, they often send scouts to go ahead of the group to find a good location.

   a. to look for **b.** to choose

B Compare your answers to Exercise A with a partner.

Use the Vocabulary

Write answers to the following questions. Use the words in bold in your answers. Then share your answers with a partner.

1. What are some positive ways to avoid **conflicts** with friends or family members?

2. What animal is the most **intelligent**, in your opinion? Give examples of this animal's intelligence.

3. How important is body language in human **interaction**? Is it **a key component**? Why, or why not?

4. Libraries and study rooms should be in quiet places so students won't be distracted by noise. Is the library and/or study area in your school in a **suitable location**? Why, or why not?

5. What is the best way to **solve** serious **problems** in your community?

6. How do you feel when you have to be very **close together** with many other people in a public place such as in an elevator, on the subway, or at a concert?

THINK AND DISCUSS

Work in a small group. Use the information in the reading and your own ideas to discuss the following questions.

1. **Summarize.** How do bees decide where the best place to move their hive is?

2. **Apply knowledge.** Why do you think swarms might be more efficient if the individuals aren't particularly intelligent?

3. **Make connections.** In what situations do you think humans might behave like swarms?

Vocabulary Review

A Complete the paragraphs with the vocabulary below that you have studied in the unit.

dominant role	is in charge	reduce conflict	take over
high status	key component	suitable location	when it comes to

Chimpanzees live in groups of several dozen members. Each group has a strict hierarchy with one male having the _____. This individual _____ of the group. One of his roles is to _____ and maintain order, especially when there are problems within the group. Also, he can mate with any female he wants.

A male chimpanzee can often become a leader without using physical force. In fact, _____ group leadership, the dominant male does not even have to be the largest or strongest individual in the group. This is because a chimpanzee leader can _____ a group just by creating relationships with allies—other members of the group who support him.

Female chimpanzees have their own hierarchy within the group. In some groups, a daughter of a high-ranking mother will inherit her mother's _____. A _____ of a female's high status is being able to make decisions about food. Her responsibility is to make sure that the group will go to a _____ for finding food.

B Compare answers to Exercise A with a partner. Then discuss the following question.

What is the difference between male and female chimpanzee hierarchies?

C Complete the following sentences in a way that shows that you understand the meaning of the words in bold.

1. Parents often want to **protect** their children **from** _harm, hurt and_ .
2. The most **dramatic changes** in my life _moving to a new city_ .

3. To **solve a problem**, it can be helpful to _identify and exploit_.

4. It's difficult to **follow the rules** when you _____.

D Work with a partner and write four sentences that include any four of the vocabulary items below. You may use any verb tense and make nouns plural if you wish.

cooperate with	furthermore	in search of
from time to time	interactions between	keep watch over

Connect the Readings

A Look back at Readings 1 and 2 to complete the chart below. Put a check (✓) in the boxes to show which topics appeared in each reading. Note that some topics appeared in both readings.

	Reading 1	Reading 2
1. Family groups		
2. Group behavior		
3. Leadership		
4. Breeding and parenting		
5. Cooperation between individuals		
6. Competition between individuals		
7. Intelligence		
8. Female and male roles		
9. Communication between individuals		
10. Using knowledge of animal behavior to help humans		

B With a partner or in a small group, compare answers to Exercise A. Then discuss the following questions.

1. Find the topics that appear in both readings. In which reading was each topic more important?

2. Of all of the topics listed in Exercise A, which was the most interesting to you? Why?

C Discuss the following questions with a partner. Use your understanding of the readings and your own ideas.

1. Which group of animals discussed in Reading 1 have swarm-like behavior as described in Reading 2?

2. Which of the animals discussed in Readings 1 and 2 sound the most intelligent to you? Give reasons for your answers.

3. Think about cooperation and competition in your classroom. In which situations do you cooperate with other students? In which situations do you compete with other students?

Making News

Boys reading newspapers
in 1936 in Paris, France

FOCUS
1. How often do you read, listen to, or watch the news?
2. Do you prefer getting news from the Internet, radio, TV, or a newspaper? Explain your answer.

Academic Vocabulary

enormous	to identify	a source
to evaluate	professional	widespread

Multiword Vocabulary

to be on the scene	to point out that
to come to the aid of	to tell the truth
to learn a lesson	to tell the whole story

Reading Preview

Ⓐ **Preview.** Skim Reading 1 by reading the first and last sentence of each paragraph. Then check (✓) four topics below that you think might be in this reading.

_____ **1.** The job reporters do

_____ **2.** Ordinary people who report news stories

_____ **3.** Cell phones that help people report the news

_____ **4.** The causes of earthquakes

_____ **5.** Ordinary people who report news stories can help in disasters

_____ **6.** False news reports on the Internet

Ⓑ **Topic vocabulary.** The following words appear in Reading 1. Look at the words and answer the questions with a partner.

destruction	posted	survivor
earthquake	rescuer	tsunami
journalist	report	victim
online		

1. Which words refer to how the news is delivered?

2. How are the words *earthquake, tsunami,* and *destruction* related?

3. Which words refer to people who are often involved in or affected by a natural disaster?

Ⓒ **Predict.** What do you think this reading will be about? Discuss each word in Exercise B and predict how it may relate to the reading.

Most news comes from professional journalists. But sometimes we get amazing eyewitness reports from average citizens who just happen to be in the right place at the right time!

Accidental Reporters

Tourists take photos of each other in flooded Saint Mark's square in Venice, Italy.

A tsunami wave hits the beach on Penang Island, Malaysia in December 2004. The photo was taken by a tourist, Eric Skitzi.

A strong earthquake occurred near Indonesia in December 2004. It created a huge wave called a tsunami. The tsunami hit[1] many coastal communities around the Indian Ocean in places such as Indonesia, Thailand, India, and Sri Lanka. It killed more than 230,000 people. How did the world learn of this event? Not from professional journalists. The first reports came from citizen journalists. These were ordinary people, such as tourists, who were on the scene when the tsunami hit. They took videos and photos with their cell phones. They sent emails, and they posted their stories online.

An American tourist, Rick Von Feldt, was on the island of Phuket in Thailand when the tsunami hit. He wrote an email about what happened. "We all stood there, stunned,"[2] he wrote. "People came running up the road. . . . 'Water—the water,' they were crying." Then Von Feldt described how an 18-foot (5.5-meter) wall of water poured onto the beach, and how in just a few seconds, everything and everyone was

1

2

---

[1] *hit:* struck; happened in

[2] *stunned:* feeling surprised or shocked

covered with water and then carried out to sea.

Von Feldt was one of many people who became accidental[3] reporters of the disaster. TV networks and major newspapers used the messages and pictures of these ordinary people. Jay Rosen, a journalism professor at New York University, explains that videos of the event told the whole story. You didn't need any background information.[4] "You watch this wave and the destruction, and that's the story," he said. Other experts point out that stories from citizen journalists are often especially interesting because of the personal aspect of their reports.

3

Citizen journalists can provide the public with information. But they can do more. For example, phone reports can help rescue workers find disaster victims who may be seriously injured. After an earthquake hit eastern Turkey in 2011, cell phone reports helped rescuers. They quickly came to the aid of a young survivor who was under a collapsed building. In other cases, citizen journalists have called the police when there were robberies or other crimes in a disaster area.

4

Most stories from citizen journalists are accurate. The reporters are not professionals, but they tell the truth. However, you cannot trust all stories on the Internet, so you often have to evaluate the information you read very carefully. For example, when news organizations were reporting the 2004 tsunami, they used pictures of an enormous wave that they found on the Internet. However, they soon found out that the pictures actually showed a wave on a Chinese river in 2002. Who posted the pictures? No one knew. The news organizations learned a lesson. They had to check their sources more carefully.

5

President Kennedy in Dallas moments before being shot.

THE ZAPRUDER FILM

One of the first pieces of accidental reporting was a short film of the assassination of President John F. Kennedy in 1963. A man named Abraham Zapruder came to Dallas, Texas, to see and film the president as his car drove by. Zapruder found a platform to stand on so he was above the others. As Kennedy's car approached, Zapruder turned on his movie camera. Zapruder's film was only 27 seconds long, but Zapruder caught the moment Kennedy got shot. Zapruder was just an ordinary person in the right place at the right time.

They sent out apologies for the false reports. False reports also appear on social media sites such as Facebook and Twitter. Fake[5] pictures of sharks swimming in the Hudson River appeared on Twitter during the 2012 hurricane in New York.

The main tool of citizen journalists is the cell phone. Cell phone use is widespread, and smartphone use is increasing, too. Nowadays, almost everyone owns a cell phone or a smartphone, and almost every phone has a camera. By 2012, more than half of the people in the world had cell phones. In the United States, China, and other large countries, the figure was more than 80 percent. As more and more people own cell phones, we may face a new problem. There may be too much news from too many sources.

6

There is no doubt that, in the future, more citizen journalists will report breaking news stories. It is also true that we will need better skills to identify which sources are reliable and which are not.

7

---

[3] *accidental:* not planned

[4] *backround information:* facts that explain an event or situation

---

[5] *fake:* not real, but created to look real

READING COMPREHENSION

Big Picture

A The following statements are the main ideas for paragraphs 2, 3, 5, and 7 in Reading 1. Write the correct paragraph number next to its main idea.

_____ **1.** Not all stories from citizen journalists are accurate.

_____ **2.** A tourist wrote a dramatic email as the tsunami hit.

_____ **3.** Citizen journalists' reports of the tsunami were interesting because they told a personal story.

_____ **4.** We will see more citizen journalism, some unreliable, in the future.

B Compare answers to Exercise A with a partner. Then complete the main ideas of paragraphs 4, 6, and the short extra reading, "The Zapruder Film," on page 131.

1. Citizen journalists can help _____ find victims, too.

2. Use of the main tool of the citizen journalist, the _____, is increasing.

3. The Zapruder film _____ accidental reporting.

Close-Up

A Decide which of the following statements are true or false according Reading 1 and "The Zapruder Film." Write *T* (True) or *F* (False) next to each one.

_____ **1.** Rick Von Feldt was a professional journalist.

_____ **2.** Jay Rosen knows a lot about citizen journalism.

_____ **3.** Some news organizations posted the wrong picture of the wave in Thailand.

_____ **4.** The Internet helped rescue workers in eastern Turkey.

_____ **5.** An earthquake hit Turkey in 2011.

_____ **6.** More than 50 percent of the world's population had cell phones in 2012.

_____ **7.** Professional journalists in Thailand posted the first videos of the tsunami.

_____ **8.** Most stories from citizen journalists are not accurate.

_____ **9.** Zapruder was a reporter who came to Dallas in 1963 to film President Kennedy.

B Work with a partner or in a small group. Change the false statements in Exercise A to make them true.

Zapruder's camera

Reading Skill

Ⓐ Find and read the quotations below from Reading 1. Then answer the questions.

1. *"People came running up the road. . . . 'Water—the water,' they were crying."* (Par. 2)

   a. Who is the source of this quotation? _____

   b. Is this source believable? Why, or why not? _____

   c. Does the quotation support the main idea? _____

2. *"You watch this wave and the destruction, and that's the story."* (Par. 3)

   a. Who is the source of the quotation? _____

   b. Is the source believable? Why, or why not? _____

   c. Does the quotation support the main idea? _____

Ⓑ Work with a partner. Below are two new quotations that could be added to Reading 1. Check (✓) the correct paragraph in which the quotation would appear.

1. *"We are still trying to find out who posted the photos online, and we are doing everything to make sure we never make a mistake like this again," said the owner of the newspaper.*

   _____ Par. 4   _____ Par. 5   _____ Par. 6

2. *"I thought for sure I was going to die," one victim said after the rescue workers pulled him to safety.*

   _____ Par. 4   _____ Par. 5   _____ Par. 6

VOCABULARY PRACTICE

Academic Vocabulary

Ⓐ Find the words in bold in Reading 1. Use the context to help you match each word to the correct definition.

_____ **1. professional** (Par. 1)   **a.** say who or what something or someone is

_____ **2. evaluate** (Par. 5)   **b.** relating to work that requires special training

_____ **3. enormous** (Par. 5)   **c.** extremely large; huge

_____ **4. sources** (Par. 5)   **d.** existing or happening over a large area

_____ **5. widespread** (Par. 6)   **e.** things—such as people or books—that provide information

_____ **6. identify** (Par. 7)   **f.** decide how good or bad something or someone is

B Choose an academic word from Exercise A to complete each of the following sentences. Notice and learn the words in bold because they often appear with the academic words.

1. My father was not a(n) _____ **photographer,** but he always took excellent photos.

2. Many people use television as one of their **major** _____ for news.

3. When you are doing research, _____ **information** as you read and decide if it is useful.

4. The earthquake caused _____ **damage** throughout the area.

5. The police often use fingerprints to _____ **suspects.** With this information, they can learn who the people are and if they committed the crime.

6. We see a(n) _____ **amount** of information on the Internet, and not all of it is believable.

Multiword Vocabulary

A Find the words in bold in Reading 1. Then write the words that come before and/or after them to complete the multiword vocabulary.

1. were _____ _____ **scene** (Par. 1)

2. _____ **the** _____ **story** (Par. 3)

3. point _____ **that** (Par. 3)

4. _____ **to the** _____ **of** (Par. 4)

5. tell the _____ (Par. 5)

6. _____ **a lesson** (Par. 5)

B Complete the following sentences with the correct multiword vocabulary from Exercise A. In some cases, you need to change the verb form.

1. When disasters such as hurricanes strike, volunteers often _____ people who are affected so they can help them with injuries and other problems.

2. It's important to _____ when the police question you. If you lie, you might get into trouble.

3. The news report about the earthquake didn't _____. Many facts were left out.

4. When the fire happened, the firefighters _____ immediately. They arrived within 15 minutes of the call.

5. Making an embarrassing mistake is one way to _____. If you feel bad enough, you won't repeat your behavior.

6. Experiencd reporters _____ no one source can give you a complete picture. They say it's a good idea to get information from several sources.

A young girl in Sri Lanka stands in the ruins of her home, destroyed by the tsunami of December 24, 2004.

Use the Vocabulary

Write answers to the following questions. Use the words in bold in your answers. Then share your answers with a partner.

1. **Evaluate** a news story you heard in the past week. Did it **tell the whole story**? How do you know? What was the **source** of the story?

2. Have you ever **come to the aid of** a person who was in trouble? What happened? How did you help?

3. Think of a recent experience that helped you **learn a lesson**. What was the experience? What did you learn?

4. What kinds of documents do we use to **identify** ourselves?

5. Are any other **professional** jobs (besides journalism) changing due to the Internet and social media? What are they? How are they changing?

THINK AND DISCUSS

Work in a small group. Use the information in the reading and your own ideas to discuss the following questions.

1. **Identify differences.** What is the difference between a report from a citizen journalist and a report from a professional journalist? How do you know the difference?

2. **Express an opinion.** Imagine a natural disaster has happened. Would you rather learn about it from a professional journalist or a citizen journalist? Explain your answer.

3. **Analyze.** When is it better to get news from citizen journalists? When is it better to get news from professional journalists?

Academic Vocabulary

access	to convince	media
awareness	eventually	a site

Multiword Vocabulary

to get something off the ground	to tear something down
to paint a picture of	a way of life
to take pride in	a wide range of

Reading Preview

A **Preview.** Read the title of Reading 2. Look at the photos on pages 136–139 and read their captions. Then discuss the following questions with a partner or in a small group.

1. Where is Kibera?

2. What kind of place is Kibera?

3. What is the man in the photo on page 138 listening to?

B **Topic vocabulary.** The following words appear in Reading 2. Look at the words and answer the questions with a partner.

community	residents	unhealthy
dangerous	set up	unsafe
donate	train	volunteer
publicize		

1. Which words relate to people living in a particular place?

2. Which words describe a place negatively?

3. Which words relate to running and funding a big project?

C **Predict.** What do you think this reading will be about? Discuss each word in Exercise B and predict how it may relate to the reading.

It is not always easy for a poor community in a distant part of the world to tell its story. Learn how the people of Kibera in Kenya were able to let the world know about their way of life.

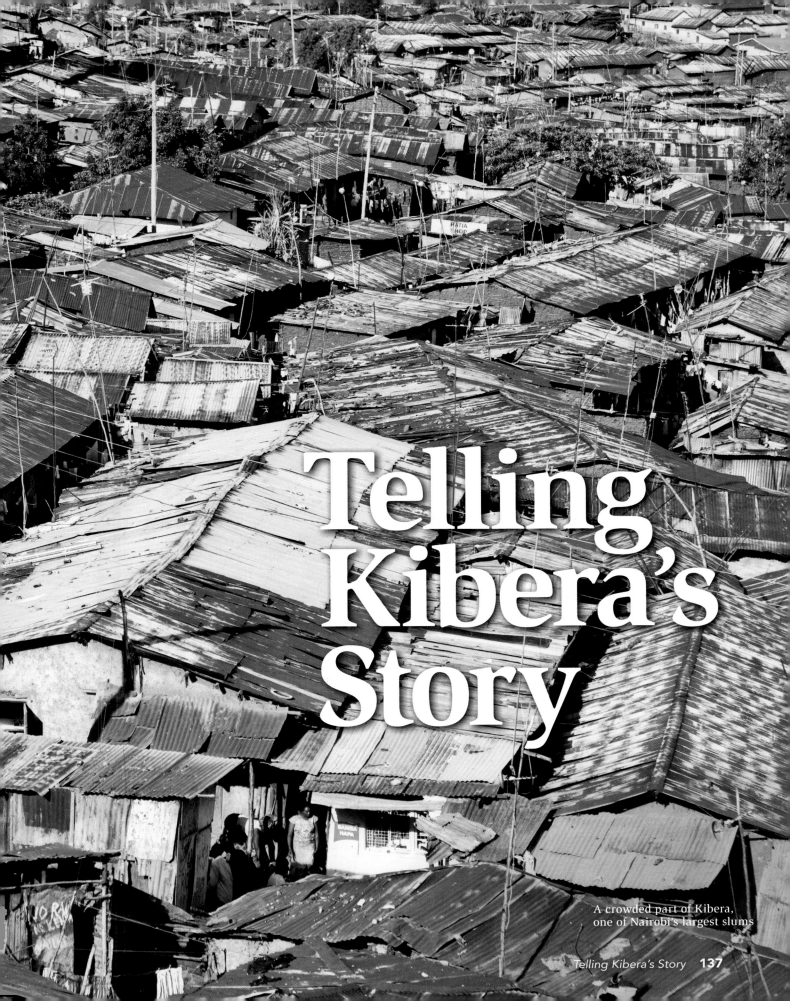

Telling Kibera's Story

A crowded part of Kibera, one of Nairobi's largest slums

News stories tell us about everything from natural disasters to celebrities' lives. But what *don't* we hear about on the news? Are there stories of everyday people that we should also hear about? One American student doing volunteer work in the Kenyan slum[1] of Kibera thought there was.

Kibera is a few miles from the center of Nairobi, the capital of Kenya. Some people who live there are hungry. Clean water is hard to get, diseases are common, and most buildings are unsafe. Life is so bad in Kibera that the Kenyan government had plans to tear it down eventually. But was tearing down Kibera really the best solution for its residents? Most Kiberans didn't think so because they didn't want to lose their lifelong home. Other Kenyans thought tearing down Kibera was a good idea because it was

> *"But was tearing down Kibera really the best solution for its residents?"*

such a dangerous and unhealthy place. However, most Kenyans did not really know what life was like in Kibera. There wasn't much news about life in Kibera. This was true even though major news media outlets such as the BBC, CNN, and the *New York Times* have offices in Nairobi. Kibera itself has just one radio station, Pamoja FM, and its weak radio signal does not even reach most parts of Nairobi.

Kyle Bullington, the American student volunteer, decided that telling Kibera's story could benefit the people who live there. Kyle saw the problems in Kibera one summer as a volunteer in a local soccer program. He went home and started working on a project to publicize Kibera's situation. He wanted the world to know what life was like there. He believed citizen journalism and video-sharing Web sites would be the best way to send out reports about Kibera. An organization called Carolina for Kibera helped Kyle. They convinced people to donate equipment

1

2

3

---

[1] *slum:* a large area of a city where the houses are in bad condition and residents are often very poor

A Kiberan listens to a local radio program about Kiberan life and local news.

Kyle spent two weeks in Kibera getting the video project off the ground. He trained some Kiberans to use the video equipment. These Kiberans became citizen journalists. They posted a number of videos on a YouTube channel created by Kyle. The videos paint a picture of life in the community. They cover a wide range of everyday activities such as Kiberans working, playing soccer, and going about their daily lives. Kyle takes pride in the Kiberans' work. "They have been making monthly posts about life in Kibera," Kyle noted online. "I hope that these videos will . . . help Kiberans raise awareness of the Kiberan way of life all around the world." 4

In the years since Kyle's visit, Kiberans have become more comfortable using technology. Many residents now own cell phones, which make connecting with the world even easier. Pamoja FM has set up a system that allows residents to call in and tell a reporter about the latest news events. The reporter often uses a cell phone to report back to the radio station. Pamoja FM sometimes lets Kibera residents speak on the radio themselves. As people have more access to technology, the outside world will hear a lot more about what is happening in Kibera. In addition, it will help Kenyans make better decisions about the future of Kibera. 5

such as small digital video cameras and new laptops. In the summer of 2009, Kyle returned to Kibera to start the online video project.

READING COMPREHENSION

Big Picture

Ⓐ Choose the answer that best completes each of the following sentences.

1. In paragraph 2, the writer shows _____.
   a. what life is like in Kibera
   b. that there are hardly any news organizations in Nairobi

2. In paragraph 3, the writer introduces _____.
   a. Kyle Bullington and describes the type of person he is
   b. Kyle Bullington and explains his role in a project

3. In paragraph 4, the writer describes _____.
   a. the videos that the Kiberans made
   b. the surprising and unusual ways that Kiberans spend their days

4. In paragraph 5, the writer shows _____.
   a. the usefulness of cell phones for the Kiberans
   b. how news organizations are helping Kibera

B Read the following statements. Check (✓) the statement that best expresses the main idea of the *whole* reading.

_____ **1.** News media outlets should report more local stories.

_____ **2.** Kibera is a dangerous and unhealthy place to live.

_____ **3.** Citizen journalists helped Kiberans tell their story.

_____ **4.** Kyle Bullington is a hero.

Close-Up

A Complete the following sentences in your own words.

1. Kibera is a _____ in the Kenyan city of Nairobi.

2. Pamoja FM is the only _____ in Kibera.

3. Pamoja FM doesn't even reach all parts of _____ .

4. Many people in Kenya _____ the government's plans for Kibera.

5. Kyle Bullington worked with an _____ called Carolina for Kibera.

6. People donated _____ and _____ to Kyle's project to take to Kibera.

7. Kyle helped the Kiberans make their own _____ to put online.

8. The Kiberans made videos about their _____ lives.

B Compare answers to Exercise A with a partner. Then go back to the reading and underline the information in the passage that gave you each answer.

Reading Skill

Identifying Supporting Examples

Good writers make general statements and then support them with specific examples. Successful readers look for these relationships in each paragraph.

General Statement	Specific Example
Major news media outlets have offices in Nairobi.	BBC, CNN, and the New York Times
There are now new ways to report the news.	Citizen journalism

Sometimes, a signal word or phrase indicates an example. Some signal words or phrases are *such as, like,* and *for example.*

> *Major news media outlets such as the BBC and the New York Times have offices there.*

At other times, there is no signal word or phrase, but the context tells you that the writer is using an example.

> *There are now new ways to report the news. Citizen journalism is one of those ways, and it is changing the news we hear about.*

A Match the general statements in the left column with the specific examples that support them from the right column. Write the letter of the example next to the statement it supports.

General Statements

_____ **1.** Not much news from Kibera reaches the outside world.

_____ **2.** There is news to report about Kibera.

_____ **3.** Kibera is an unhealthy place.

_____ **4.** People donated technology.

_____ **5.** Kibera's videos show everyday life.

Specific Examples

a. video cameras and laptops

b. plans to tear down Kibera

c. radio signal doesn't reach many parts of Nairobi

d. playing soccer and working

e. clean water is hard to get

B Compare answers to Exercise A with a partner.

VOCABULARY PRACTICE

Academic Vocabulary

A Find the words in bold in Reading 2. Use the context and the sentences below to help you match each word to the correct definition.

_____ **1.** It was a very long and cold winter, but **eventually** (Par. 2) spring came and all the flowers started to bloom.

_____ **2.** The world's **media** (Par. 2) are covering the big game tonight. People will be able to watch it or listen to it wherever they are.

_____ **3.** It's getting easier to create your own Web **sites** (Par. 3).

_____ **4.** Amy **convinced** (Par. 3) me to visit her in Miami this summer, but now I want to change my plans. I think it will be too hot there in the summer.

_____ **5.** It's difficult to raise **awareness** (Par. 4) of problems that people don't want to talk about.

_____ **6.** Many libraries offer **access** (Par. 5) to the Internet for people who don't have **access** to the Internet at home.

a. persuaded or made someone change his or her mind about something

b. the ability to see or use something

c. in the end, often after many delays

d. knowledge about something

e. places on the Internet

f. television, radio, newspaper, the Internet, etc.

B Find the words in bold in Reading 2. Then circle the word that comes before and/or after it in the reading.

1. access _____   **a.** to   **b.** of

2. _____ **awareness**   **a.** make   **b.** raise

3. convinced _____   **a.** people   **b.** buildings

4. media _____   **a.** newspapers   **b.** outlets

5. _____ **sites**   **a.** Web   **b.** family

Multiword Vocabulary

(A) Find the multiword vocabulary in bold in Reading 2. Use the context to help you complete each definition.

1. If someone plans to **tear** something **down** (Par. 2), he or she is going to _____ .
   a. start it again   **b.** destroy it

2. When you are **getting** something **off the ground** (Par. 4), you _____ .
   a. are starting a project or business
   b. are moving something from one place to another

3. When people **paint a picture of** something (Par. 4), they _____ .
   a. take a photo of it   **b.** give a description of it

4. If something covers **a wide range of** something (Par. 4), it _____ .
   a. talks about a large number of different things
   b. it repeats a lot of the same information as something else

5. If someone **takes pride in** something (Par. 4), he or she _____ .
   a. takes responsibility for it
   b. thinks it's good and wants to show it to people

6. When people talk about their **way of life** (Par. 4), they are describing _____ .
   a. their normal routines   **b.** their average family size

(B) Complete the following sentences with the correct multiword vocabulary from Exercise A. In some cases, you need to change the verb or noun form.

1. The college offers _____ courses from accounting to zoology.

2. It makes children happy when they see that that their parents
_____ the things they do.

3. When a government decides to _____ old apartment buildings, it can be very difficult for the residents to find new new places to live.

4. I read a great book about life in the 1800s. The author _____
life without electricity, cars, or good medical treatment.

5. It can take a lot of money to _____ a new project _____ .

6. When people move to a new country, they often make changes to their

_____ .

Use the Vocabulary

Write answers to the following questions. Use the words in bold in your answers. Then share your answers with a partner.

1. Imagine that you want some friends from far away to visit you. How would you **convince** them to visit?

2. What types of **media** do you use most often? Why, and what kind of information do you get from each type?

3. Think about someone you know who has a different **way of life** from your life. How is it different?

A Kiberan tomato seller

4. What is something that you **take pride in**? Describe it and explain why you **take pride in** it.

5. What organizations raise **awareness** of problems in the world? What kinds of problems do they raise awareness of?

6. What **sites** do you visit the most on the Internet? Why?

7. If you were the mayor of a big city you know of, what buildings or areas would you want to **tear down**? Give reasons for your choice.

8. Do you know a television show or a movie that **paints a picture of** a different time, place, or way of life? What is it and what does it describe?

THINK AND DISCUSS

Work in a small group. Use the information in the reading and your own ideas to discuss the following questions.

1. **Infer information.** What do you think were the easiest parts and the most challenging parts of Kyle Bullington's project? Explain your ideas.

2. **Apply information.** What do you think might be the hardest adjustment for Kiberans to make after the government tears Kibera down? What ways do you think the government should help them?

3. **Relate to personal experience.** What things in your life or community do you think it would be good for other people to know about? How would you use citizen journalism to do that?

Vocabulary Review

A Complete the paragraph with the vocabulary below that you have studied in the unit.

evaluate information	media outlets	point out that	take pride in
major source	on the scene of	professional journalists	a wide range of

    Television is a _____ 1 of news for many people. _____ 2 such as TV broadcasting companies rely on _____ 3 to supply them with news stories. So, what makes a good journalist? First, a good journalist should get a lot of information about an event or situation. To do this, a journalist usually interviews _____ 4 people. This way, he or she can tell the whole story, and not just one side, or opinion of it. A good journalist is also _____ 5 a breaking news story as quickly as possible. This means the journalist can report the story as soon as possible. In fact, professional journalists often _____ 6 being the first to report a story. A journalist's job can be very interesting and exciting because he or she often gets to travel around the world. However, it is important to _____ 7 a journalist's job can also be very dangerous. Reporting a breaking news story often means being in places where there are wars, earthquakes, or tsunamis. Being aware of the situation around them is crucial for journalists in order to avoid getting hurt or killed. Being a good journalist is not easy. It requires a lot of hard work, an ability to _____ 8 carefully, and a willingness to take risks.

B Compare answers to Exercise A with a partner. Then discuss the following questions.

What are two things that a good journalist does? Why is it hard to be a good journalist?

C Complete the following sentences in a way that shows that you understand the meaning of the words in bold.

1. Journalists should **tell the whole story** because _____.

2. Rescuers who **come to the aid of** disaster victims are _____.

3. I **learned** an important **lesson** when _____.

4. My favorite Web **site** is _____.

D Work with a partner and write four sentences that include any four of the vocabulary items below.

access to	enormous damage	tell the truth
convince people	tear something down	a way of life

Connect the Readings

A Look back at Readings 1 and 2 to complete the chart below. Work with a partner and write brief notes about each place in the chart.

	Kibera	Phuket
What are/were citizen journalists reporting?		
Describe the type of citizen journalists.		
What are the benefits of using cell phones?		
What media outlets used reports from citizen journalists?		
What were the benefits of having citizen journalists?		

B With a partner or in a small group, compare answers to Exercise A. Then discuss the following questions.

1. What are the differences in how citizen journalism happens in each reading?

2. What are the effects or benefits of citizen journalism in each reading? How are they different and how are they similar in the readings?

C Discuss the following questions with a partner. Use your understanding of the readings and your own ideas.

1. Have you ever taken a photo or a video of a news story? If so, what did it show? If not, describe a situation when you would take a photo or video?

2. In both readings, the media sometimes use citizen journalists. What is your opinion of this practice? Do you think the media should pay citizen journalists? Give reasons for your opinion.

Noise
and
Light

Fireworks welcome in the
new year in Singapore.

FOCUS

1. What types of pollution affect Earth?

2. Do you think noise and light are types of pollution? Why, or why not?

Academic Vocabulary

constant	to maintain	a regulation
to deprive	a period	to reproduce

Multiword Vocabulary

to come to the conclusion that	an occupational hazard
to consist of	to pose a threat
to drive someone crazy	to put up with

A child covers his ears because of the noise from old bikes, Finland.

Reading Preview

Ⓐ **Preview.** Skim Reading 1 by reading the first sentence of each paragraph. Then discuss the following questions with a partner or in a small group.

1. What is noise pollution?

2. What problems might too much noise cause?

3. Are there any solutions to noise pollution?

Ⓑ **Topic vocabulary.** The following words appear in Reading 1. Look at the words and answer the questions with a partner.

barriers	memory	sirens
earplugs	migraines	soundproofing
medicine	roar	vibrations

1. Which words are related to sounds?

2. Which words suggest the reading will mention health problems?

3. How are the words *soundproofing*, *barriers*, and *earplugs* related?

Ⓒ **Predict.** What do you think this reading will be about? Discuss each word in Exercise B and predict how it may relate to the reading.

What problems can everyday noise—music, traffic, or airplanes cause? Read about the effects of too much noise on people, animals, and nature. Then learn about some possible solutions.

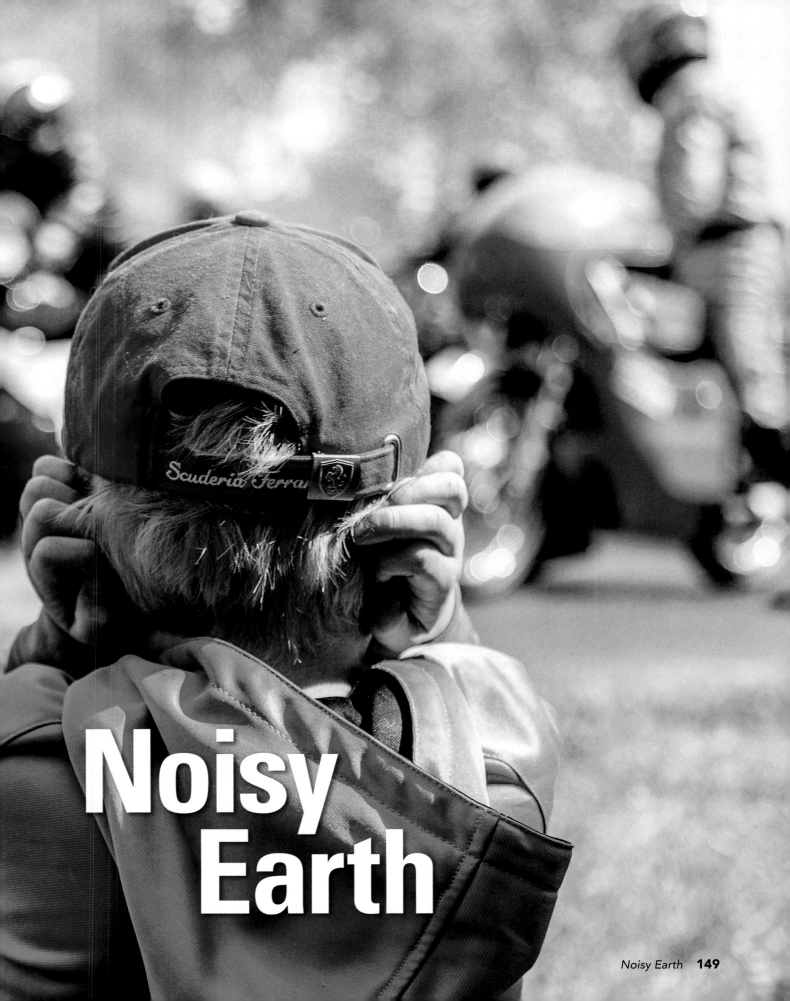

Noisy
Earth

When we think of pollution, we usually think of harmful toxins[1] in the environment. For example, air pollution is contaminated[2] air that can be dangerous to breathe. Water pollution is contaminated water that can be dangerous to drink. But there's another kind of pollution. It's noise. And it can be just as harmful to livings things as other types of pollution.

Noise pollution consists of loud sounds in the environment that are disruptive.[3] Just like other types of pollution, noise pollution is caused by humans. Noise pollution is mainly a problem in cities. Car alarm sirens, construction work, the roar of engines, and loud music are just a few examples of noise pollution. This noise can be so annoying it drives people crazy.

Why should we be concerned about noise pollution? According to a World Health Organization report, noise can cause serious health problems. It deprives people of sleep and causes heart disease and hearing loss. These problems are an occupational hazard for people who work in noisy places. Musicians, mechanics, police officers, and airport workers all have to put up with noise pollution. As a result, they suffer from hearing loss. For example, Subir Malik of the rock band Parikrama has been a musician for over 25 years. Malik doesn't hear well in one ear. "In our early years, there was no knowledge of [ear] protection," he says. Today, Malik wears earplugs when he performs. Even servers in restaurants can suffer health problems, according to a *New York*

> *"Physical health problems are just some of the effects of noise pollution."*

Times article. The article talks about a server at Lavo, a restaurant in New York City. The server takes medicine for the migraines she gets from the constant noise in the restaurant.

Physical health problems are just some of the effects of noise pollution. Studies show that loud noise affects learning ability and memory, too. Scientists at the Central China Normal University in Hubei, China, taught mice to travel through a maze.[4] Some mice did the maze with moderate noise while other mice did the maze with no noise. The experiment lasted for a period of six weeks. The mice with moderate

---

[4] *maze:* a place that is difficult to find your way through

Figure 1: How Ocean Noise Can Affect Whales and Fish

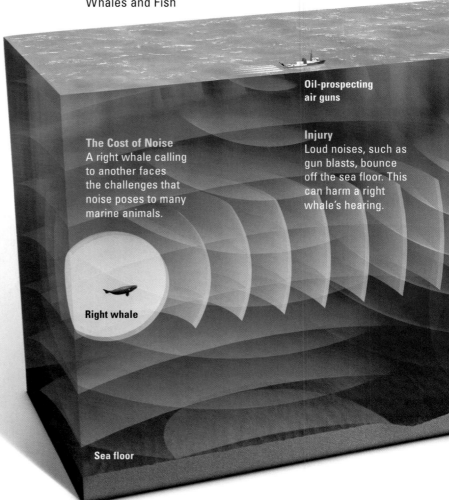

Oil-prospecting air guns

The Cost of Noise
A right whale calling to another faces the challenges that noise poses to many marine animals.

Injury
Loud noises, such as gun blasts, bounce off the sea floor. This can harm a right whale's hearing.

Right whale

Sea floor

---

[1] *toxins:* poisonous or harmful substances

[2] *contaminated:* made dirty and harmful from dirt, chemicals, or radiation

[3] *disruptive:* preventing something from continuing in the normal way

noise had more trouble learning and remembering the maze. The study showed that even moderate noise can affect learning and memory.

Noise poses a threat to animals in nature as 5 well. Noise can cause animals to die from lack of food. For example, some types of birds cannot find food in areas that have bad noise pollution. Noise affects marine animals, too. Whales, for example, produce sounds in order to communicate with each other. Noises in the ocean from ships and other human activities can interrupt whale communication. The noises can also affect the ability of whales to find a mate, which could reduce whale populations (see Figure 1). In addition, a researcher at Barcelona's Technical University of Catalonia found that noise pollution can cause physical harm to marine animals. The researcher found several dead giant squids off the coast of Spain. He came to the conclusion that vibrations from the guns of naval ships in the area tore holes in the squids' statocysts. Statocysts are organs behind the squids eyes that help them maintain balance. Damage to the statocysts made it impossible for the squids to swim, eat, or reproduce, and they died.

Noise pollution is a serious problem, but 6 there are some solutions. Volvo, a company that

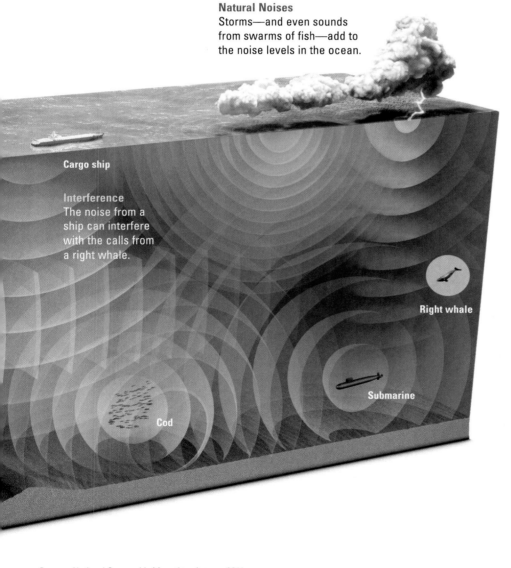

Natural Noises
Storms—and even sounds from swarms of fish—add to the noise levels in the ocean.

Cargo ship

Interference
The noise from a ship can interfere with the calls from a right whale.

Right whale

Submarine

Cod

260 Oil-prospecting air guns, lightning
250

Sounds above 170 decibels (dB) can injure marine animals.

200

192 Cargo ship

170 Right whale

150 *Sounds between 120–170 dB can disturb animal behavior.*

105 Cod
100 95 Submarine

80 Wind, rain

50

0 dB

The higher the decibel level, the more likely a sound is to harm animals. A few sources are shown here.

Source: National Geographic Magazine, January 2011

Noise barrier on the Taipei Metro (MRT)

walls along highways—can also reduce traffic noise. A noise barrier covered with plants along the highway near Copenhagen Airport dramatically reduced noise for nearby apartment dwellers. Companies now also make products that reduce noise in factories. For example, some machines in factories have parts that make the machines shake less and make less noise.

Countries around the 7 world recognize that noise pollution is a real problem. Many government agencies already control noise from trucks and buses. They also have laws that require buildings to have

makes engines, developed a quieter truck engine. The engine produces four times less noise than traditional trucks do. Noise barriers—thick soundproofing. With these health and safety regulations and increased awareness, we may be able to live in a quieter world.

READING COMPREHENSION

Big Picture

A Choose the answer that best completes each of the following sentences.

1. The reading discusses _____ of noise pollution.
   a. only the problems
   b. both the problems and solutions

2. According to the reading, noise pollution is _____ other types of pollution.
   a. as serious as
   b. more serious than

3. The reading defines noise pollution as loud sounds that are _____.
   a. natural and caused by humans
   b. caused by humans only

4. According to the reading, noise pollution causes _____ for humans.
   a. mental and physical problems
   b. mainly physical problems

5. According to the reading, noise pollution is also a problem for _____.
   a. plants
   b. animals

B Compare answers to Exercise A with a partner. Then discuss what you think the main idea of Reading 1 is.

Close-Up

A Scan Reading 1 to find answers to the following questions. In some cases, more than one answer is correct.

1. What are three examples of noise pollution?

_____, _____, and _____

2. What are three health problems that noise pollution can cause?

_____, _____, and _____

3. What are three jobs in which noise is an occupational hazard?

_____, _____, and _____

4. What two problems can even moderate noise cause?

_____ and _____

5. What are two kinds of animals that are affected by noise pollution?

_____ and _____

6. What were squids unable to do after they were harmed by noise pollution?

_____, _____, or _____

7. What is one solution to noisy highways? _____

B Compare answers to Exercise A with a partner. What other solutions to the problem of noise pollution does Reading 1 mention?

Reading Skill

Evaluating Sources

As you saw in Unit 7, writers often use quotations from people to support their ideas. Writers sometimes quote from other sources, too. These sources could be newspapers, Web sites, and scientific studies. Good readers pay attention to whether the sources are believable in a reading passage. Evaluating a source's qualifications can help you judge the quality of the reading. As you read, ask yourself, "Is this information from a good source?"

A Answer the following questions about the sources in Reading 1. Write the letter of the source next to the question.

_____ **1.** What source says that noise deprives people of sleep and causes heart disease and hearing loss? (Par. 3)

_____ **2.** What source talks about the effect of not wearing ear protection? (Par. 3)

_____ **3.** What source says that servers in restaurants suffer from health problems? (Par. 3)

_____ **4.** What source did an experiment on the effects of noise on learning and memory? (Par. 4)

_____ **5.** What source came to a conclusion about noise pollution and marine animals? (Par. 5)

a. a newspaper article

b. a university researcher

c. an official report

d. an experienced musician

e. a group of scientists

B With a partner, discuss why each source in Exercise A is a good source.

VOCABULARY PRACTICE

Academic Vocabulary

A Find the words in bold in Reading 1. Use the context to help you match each word to the correct definition.

_____ **1. deprives** (Par. 3)   **a.** rules

_____ **2. constant** (Par. 3)   **b.** keep at the same level

_____ **3. period** (Par. 4)   **c.** takes something necessary or important away from someone

_____ **4. maintain** (Par. 5)   **d.** length of time

_____ **5. reproduce** (Par. 5)   **e.** have babies

_____ **6. regulations** (Par. 7)   **f.** happening all the time

B Choose an academic word from Exercise A to complete each of the following sentences. Notice and learn the words in bold because they often appear with the academic words.

1. Governments often develop **safety** _____ to protect workers. Some of these rules may include wearing earplugs or hard hats to protect workers who have dangerous jobs.

2. Living near a very busy highway with nonstop traffic can cause physical and emotional problems due to the _____ **exposure** to loud noise.

3. Exposing animals to noise over a **long** _____ of time can interrupt their communication and their ability to find food.

4. Some species of animals are in danger because noise pollution is affecting their **ability to** _____. As a result, there are fewer and fewer of them.

5. A person's ability to _____ **a healthy lifestyle** depends on many factors. Sometimes staying healthy is related to your income and where you live.

6. Stress _____ **people of** sleep. People who do not get enough sleep often suffer from health problems such as obesity and heart disease.

Multiword Vocabulary

A Find the words in bold in Reading 1. Then write the words that come before and/or after them to complete the multiword vocabulary.

1. **consists** _____ (Par. 2)

2. **drives people** _____ (Par. 2)

3. **occupational** _____ (Par. 3)

4. **put** _____ **with** (Par. 3)

5. _____ **a threat** (Par. 5)

6. _____ _____ **the conclusion that** (Par. 5)

B Complete the following sentences with the correct multiword vocabulary from Exercise A. Use the words in parentheses to help you.

1. Workers don't have to _____ (tolerate) a dangerous work environment. There are ways to report dangers on the job.

2. When a neighbors' loud music _____ (makes them feel very upset), the best thing they can do is talk to the neighbors about it.

3. One solution to airport noise _____ (includes) changing landing and takeoff times.

4. After the researchers completed the experiment, they _____ (made a decision based on facts) noise pollution can affect people's ability to learn and remember new information.

5. Hearing loss can be a(n) _____ (a job-related danger) for musicians unless they wear earplugs.

6. Climate change can _____ (be a source of danger) to animals and plants. For example, polar bears are losing their habitats because higher temperatures are melting the ice where they live.

Use the Vocabulary

Write answers to the following questions. Use the words in bold in your answers. Then share your answers with a partner.

1. What suggestions do you have if noise is **depriving** someone of sleep?

2. Would you **put up with** a neighbor's loud music? If not, what would you do about it?

3. What is one thing a close friend does that really **drives** you **crazy**?

4. Are **occupational hazards posing a threat to** anyone you know? Explain your answer.

5. What activities does your typical weekend **consist of**?

6. What is one **regulation** from your school, your home, your job, or your city that you would change if you could? Explain why you would change it.

THINK AND DISCUSS

Work in a small group. Use the information in the reading and your own ideas to discuss the following questions.

1. **Relate to personal experience.** What types of noise pollution exist in your community?

2. **Evaluate.** What noise pollution solutions that you read about in Reading 1 would work best for your community?

3. **Apply knowledge.** If you worked at a job where you were at risk for certain dangers (e.g., burns, contamination, hearing loss), what would you do about your situation?

Academic Vocabulary

committed	injured	to migrate
to function	major	a pattern

Multiword Vocabulary

to emerge from	to light up
from up to (distance) away	a link between
to interfere with	to lose one's way

Reading Preview

Ⓐ Preview. Skim Reading 2 by reading the first paragraph on page 158 and the first and last sentence of each paragraph. Then make a list of four things you remember. Compare lists with a partner.

_____

_____

_____

_____

Ⓑ Topic vocabulary. The following words appear in Reading 2. Look at the words and answer the questions with a partner.

artificial	moonlit	species
cancer	obesity	streetlights
depression	plants	turtles
headlights	shines	

1. Which words relate to light?
2. Which words refer to living things?
3. Which words are related to health?

Ⓒ Predict. What do you think this reading will be about? Discuss each word in Exercise B and predict how it may relate to the reading.

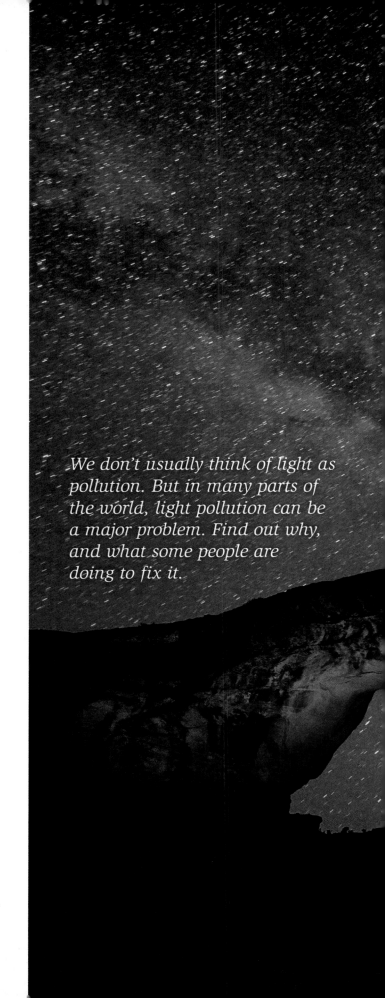

We don't usually think of light as pollution. But in many parts of the world, light pollution can be a major problem. Find out why, and what some people are doing to fix it.

Our Vanishing Night

A starry night at the Natural Bridges National Monument, Utah, USA

OUR VANISHING NIGHT

Humans are diurnal. This means we function better in the daylight. In the last 200 years, in order to create more "daylight" hours, we have filled the night with artificial light. Now we can function almost as well at night as we do during the day. There are many obvious benefits to creating more productive hours. However, the amount of artificial light we now have is also causing many problems. These problems are a result of what scientists now call *light pollution*.

Light pollution, or too much artificial light, is a relatively new problem. Just 200 years ago, the idea of light pollution didn't exist. For example, imagine walking toward London on a moonlit night around 1800. At that time, the population of London was already nearly a million people. But there were no electric lights yet. From a few miles away, travelers could probably smell London before they could see it. Now, the lights of large cities light up the skies for many miles. For example, airplane pilots can see the sky glow[1] of some major cities such as Los Angeles from up to 200 miles (322 kilometers) away.

Light pollution affects many different parts of the planet. Many scientists believe that it is one of the fastest growing types of pollution. Two-thirds of the world's population lives with light pollution. Today, people in only a few parts of the world can see the stars of the night skies properly. Only one-third of the world's population can see the Milky Way[2] at all. Light pollution affects many living things from the flowering of plants to the breeding[3] of animals.

Light pollution is a terrible problem for birds. It can cause night-flying birds to crash into buildings. Scientists believe that in New York City alone 10,000 birds die or get injured in this way every year. The light night sky can also cause birds that migrate at night to lose their way. Scientists are not quite sure why these birds get lost. Some think they need to see the stars to migrate. The scientists estimate that many

Street lights of Chicago burn brightly at night under a blanket of clouds.

millions of birds in North America die or are injured each year as a result of light pollution.

Light pollution causes problems for other animals, as well. Sea turtles, for example, prefer dark beaches to build nests and lay their eggs. But dark beaches are harder and harder to find. Sea turtles have to nest on artificially lit beaches. When baby turtles emerge from their shells, their instincts tell them to crawl to the moonlit ocean. But the turtles get turned around by the headlights of cars on nearby roads or the lights of nearby buildings. In Florida alone, hundreds of thousands of baby turtles die every year.

Scientists are studying the effects of light pollution on people, too. New research has found a link between light pollution and breast cancer. One study found that in very brightly

---

[1] *sky glow:* light in the air above brightly lit towns and cities

[2] *the Milky Way:* the pale strip of light seen in the sky that consists of many stars

[3] *breeding:* the process of reproducing or making babies

lit neighborhoods, the risk of developing breast cancer was 73 percent higher than in darker neighborhoods. This may be because of changing sleep patterns. When we sleep, we naturally produce a hormone called melatonin. Melatonin can be helpful in fighting cancer. But light pollution interferes with our natural sleep patterns. As a result, we produce less melatonin. Scientists are also studying the link between unnatural sleep patterns and obesity and depression.

Although light pollution is everywhere, it is one 7 of the easiest types of pollution to fix. Light pollution happens when light shines upward into the sky. One solution is to use softer yellow lighting. Another solution is to focus all lighting downward. The town of Harmony, Florida, has covered its street lamps so all the light shines downward. Some major cities such as Toronto, Canada, are turning out more lights in their high-rise office buildings at night. Flagstaff, Arizona, has also worked hard to reduce its light pollution. In 2001, it was declared the first International Dark Sky City.

The effort to control light pollution is spreading 8 around the globe. Some countries are committed to reducing light pollution. For example, the Czech Republic has laws to prevent light pollution. Although the research on light pollution is relatively recent, there is little doubt that fixing this problem will produce great benefits.

READING COMPREHENSION

Big Picture

Ⓐ The following show the author's purpose for some of the paragraphs in Reading 2. Write the correct paragraph number next to each purpose.

_____ **1.** To explain why light pollution is a problem for birds

_____ **2.** To suggest some possible solutions to the problem

_____ **3.** To give a history of light pollution

_____ **4.** To describe how scientists are looking into the effects of light pollution on humans

_____ **5.** To show how light pollution is a global problem

_____ **6.** To describe the problems light pollution causes for sea turtles

Vocabulary Review

A Complete the paragraphs with the vocabulary below that you have studied in the unit.

consist of	occupational hazard
get injured	poses a threat
links between	put up with
a long period	safety regulations

Living with noise pollution for a long time can be very dangerous. Health problems are a well-known

_____ for people who
1
work in airports. Airport workers have used earmuffs for years so their ears

wouldn't _____ from all the noise. But scientists were never sure about
2
whether air or noise pollution was worse for people's hearts. This is because most large studies looked at the health problems of people who live near airports and near busy roads. People who live near busy roads breathe polluted air. People who live near airports, however, don't have to

_____ air that is as polluted as the air near busy roads. So by comparing the
3
number of heart attacks of people living near airports with those living near busy roads, the researchers were able to see the effects of noise pollution by itself.

The researchers looked into all the heart attack deaths of people living near airports over

_____ . The researchers were able to clearly show _____
4   5
living near airports and having heart attacks. The conclusion of the study was that the high level

of noise definitely _____ to people's hearts. The study also included some
6
suggestions for new _____ to protect the people who live near airports. They
7
_____ more sound barriers around housing areas and better soundproofing in
8
the walls of people's houses.

B Compare answers to Exercise A with a partner. Then discuss the following questions.

Do you think the research that is described in the reading was well designed? Why, or why not?

C Complete the following sentences in a way that shows that you understand the meaning of the words in bold.

1. I often **lose my way** when _____ .

2. It **drives me crazy** when _____ .

3. After baby birds **emerge from** their shells, they _____ .

4. To **maintain a healthy lifestyle**, it is important to _____ .

D Work with a partner and write four sentences that include any four of the vocabulary items below. You may use any verb tense and make nouns plural if you want.

come to the conclusion that	from up to (distance) away	major cities
constant exposure	function better	sleep patterns

Connect the Readings

A Look back at Readings 1 and 2 and compare noise and light pollution. Complete the Venn diagram by writing the letter of each fact in the correct part of the diagram.

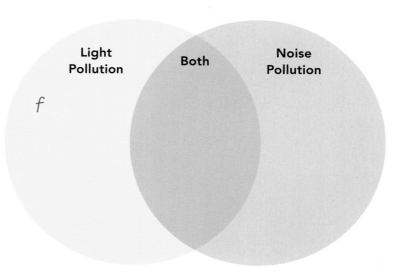

Facts

a. Causes birds to die from lack of food
b. Can cause both physical and emotional problems
c. Possibly causes cancer in humans
d. There are solutions and global efforts to control the problem
e. Can cause heart disease in humans
f. Affects a plant's ability to flower

g. Affects a whale's ability to reproduce
h. Affects people
i. Causes sea turtles to get confused and die
j. Affects animals
k. Causes direct physical harm to marine animals
l. Causes birds to get injured or lost

B With a partner or in a small group, compare answers to Exercise A. Then discuss the following questions.

1. What are the immediate effects of both types of pollution?
2. What are some long-range effects of both types of pollution?
3. What might happen if we don't solve the problem of light and noise pollution?
4. Which type of pollution seems more serious, light or noise? Explain your answer.
5. What are some solutions to the problems of light and noise pollution that are not mentioned in the two readings?

C Discuss the following questions with a partner. Use your understanding of the readings and your own ideas.

1. What are some causes of noise and light pollution that aren't mentioned in the readings?
2. Do you think some people might enjoy living in a place that always has a lot of light and noise? Why, or why not?
3. What types of pollution might improve in the future? What types might get worse? Explain your answers.

FOCUS

1. What parts of the face do you look at when you are listening to people?

2. What parts of your face do you use the most to express yourself?

Expressions

Italian football supporters before the
start of the 2006 World Cup in Germany

Academic Vocabulary

| a category | effective | to interpret |
| a culture | to focus | a reaction |

Multiword Vocabulary

to be the mirror image of	no matter whether
a facial expression	to pay attention to
in turn	wide open

Reading Preview

A Preview. Read the title of Reading 1 and look at the photos and small chart on pages 168–171. Then discuss the following questions with a partner or in a small group.

1. How are the people in the pictures feeling?

2. In your opinion, which emoticon in Figure 1 on page 171 best shows the feeling of happiness? Which one best shows the feeling of sadness?

B Topic vocabulary. The following words appear in Reading 1. Look at the words and answer the questions with a partner.

biological	fear	read
confusion	happiness	senses
disgust	physical	social
express		

1. Which words relate to emotions?

2. Which words can be used to talk about humans or their bodies?

3. Which words relate to showing and understanding expressions?

C Predict. What do you think this reading will be about? Discuss each word in Exercise B and predict how it may relate to the reading.

Does a smile mean the same thing all over the world? Are facial expressions universal? The answer is both yes and no.

A man from Rajasthan, India wearing traditional clothes and turban

In Your Face

Many people believe that facial expressions are universal. They think that a smile, for example, means the same thing everywhere in the world. Are facial expressions really universal? The answer is both yes and no. Scientists have found that facial expressions fall into two categories. Some facial expressions have physical functions.[1] These expressions are the body's natural reaction to a situation in the environment such as a smell or a surprising noise. Other facial expressions have social functions. Their function is to communicate what a person is thinking or feeling. As it turns out, expressions used for physical functions are universal, but expressions used for social functions are not.   1

Facial expressions that have a physical function are universal because we all share the same biology. Two such expressions in this category are disgust and fear. Imagine finding a very old sandwich in your refrigerator. The sandwich smells disgusting! No matter whether you're from China or Chile, you have a similar reaction to this. Eyes close, noses wrinkle,[2] and mouths tighten. Now, imagine hearing a frightening noise in the night. Again, frightened people react in a similar way all over the world. Mouths, eyes, and nostrils are wide open. Both of these sets of reactions are biological. Disgust causes people to try to shut off their senses. Eyes, noses, and mouths close up to help stop us from seeing, smelling, or even tasting the disgusting object. Fear causes the senses to work in the opposite way. It causes the senses to open up. Eyes and nostrils open wide so they are ready to catch any important information.   2

However, facial expressions that intentionally[3] communicate feelings such as happiness, anger, or confusion are different. These expressions have a social function and are not physical reactions to something in the environment. For this reason, facial expressions that have a social function can express different things in different cultures. For example, people in different cultures   3

may use smiles for different reasons. Research has found that the reason many Americans smile is the mirror image of why many Japanese people smile. According to one study, many Americans smile because they are happy. Many Japanese people, on the other hand, don't just smile when *they* are happy, but when they want *other people* to be happy.

People in different cultures may also focus   4
on different parts of the face when reading facial expressions. Studies have shown that Japanese and Chinese people usually focus more on the

---

[1] *functions:* useful jobs that things do
[2] *wrinkle:* tighten muscles and form lines on the skin
[3] *intentionally:* deliberately; on purpose

eyes. People from Western countries, on the other hand, usually focus more on the mouth. You can observe this cultural difference by looking at emoticons. A recent study compared emoticons across cultures. It showed that Japanese emoticons often use different symbols for the eyes to show happiness and sadness. The symbol for the mouth doesn't change. It is usually a straight line. In contrast, in Western emoticons, the symbols for the mouth change to show happiness and sadness. The eyes in Western emoticons rarely change.

When Americans are trying to read a facial expression, they often pay attention to someone's mouth. Some scientists say that paying attention to the eyes or the mouth to interpret an expression indicates how emotionally open a culture is. For example, according to a recent *Science Daily* article, Americans tend to express their emotions fairly openly. The part of the face that shows emotion most clearly is the mouth. It is the easiest part of the face to control and the most flexible. Not surprisingly, then, according to the article Americans pay attention to the mouth when reading facial expressions. Expressing emotion through the eyes is more difficult to do. As an example of this, it is not possible to fake the crinkling[4] around the eyes that accompanies genuine smiles. Because the eyes are more difficult to control, it makes sense that members of a culture that control their emotions more would focus on the eyes to see a true expression of emotion.

While it is easy to read disgust, pain, or fear in a face anywhere in the world, we should be more careful when interpreting other facial expressions. This may be true especially when communicating with someone from another culture. Knowing this should lead to better cultural awareness. Cultural awareness will, in turn, lead to more effective communication in our increasingly global society.

Figure 1. Emoticons from Eastern and Western Countries

	Eastern	Western
Happy	(^_^)	:)
Sad	(;_;)	:(

5

6

---

[4] *crinkling:* becoming creased or folded

READING COMPREHENSION

Big Picture

Ⓐ Choose the answer that best completes each of the following sentences according to Reading 1. Use the words from the box below.

biology	different	functions	same
cultures	eyes	mouth	universal

1. The meaning of all facial expressions is not _____.

2. Facial expressions are used for two different _____—physical and social.

3. _____ plays a role in causing some facial expressions.

4. People express some emotions—such as fear and disgust—in the _____ way all over the world.

5. People from different _____ tend to make and read some facial expressions differently.

6. The reason people smile can be _____ across cultures.

7. The facial features people use to express emotions are mainly the _____ and the _____.

B Read the following statements. Check (✓) the statement that best expresses the author's purpose for writing Reading 1.

_____ **1.** To describe the different emotions people have around the world

_____ **2.** To show how we can communicate better when we understand that not all expressions are universal

_____ **3.** To explain how people use emoticons differently

Close-Up

A Choose the word or phrase in parentheses that best completes each sentence.

1. The body's natural reaction to a situation in the environment stimulates expressions that have a (physical / social) function.

2. Expressions that communicate feelings have a (social / physical) function.

3. Nose wrinkling is often an expression of (disgust / fear).

4. Fear causes the senses to (open up / shut off).

B Compare answers to Exercise A with a partner. Then complete the chart below. Put a check (✓) in the correct column.

	Eyes	Mouth
1. The part of Japanese emoticons that generally doesn't change		
2. The part of the face Americans focus on the most		
3. The easiest part of the face to express yourself with		
4. The part of the face that can't fake a genuine smile		
5. Cultures that express themselves less openly often focus on this part of the face to read expressions		
6. The part of the face with muscles that are the hardest to control		

Reading Skill

Understanding Words That Show Contrast

Writers make clear connections between ideas by using connecting words. Good readers notice these words to help them understand these connections. In Units 3 and 8, you learned about words that show cause and effect. Writers also use words and phrases to show a contrast between two ideas, including _but, however, in contrast, while,_ and _on the other hand._

> A look of disgust is probably universal. <u>However,</u> a smile can have different meanings in different cultures.

A Read the following statements. Underline the connecting word or words that show contrast in the groups of sentences. Then answer the questions about the information in the sentences.

1. a. *As it turns out, expressions used for physical functions are universal, but expressions used for social functions are not.*

   b. Are expressions used for physical and social functions universal? _____

2. a. *While it is easy to read disgust, pain, or fear in a face anywhere in the world, we should be more careful when interpreting other facial expressions.*

   b. Is it easy to read all facial expressions? _____

3. a. *Studies have shown that Japanese and Chinese people usually focus more on the eyes. People from Western countries, on the other hand, usually focus more on the mouth.*

   b. Do all cultures focus on the same part of the face? _____

4. a. *According to one study, many Americans smile because they are happy. Many Japanese people, on the other hand, don't just smile when they are happy . . ."*

   b. Do all cultures smile when they are happy? _____

5. a. *It showed that Japanese emoticons often use different symbols for the eyes to show happiness and sadness. The symbol for the mouth doesn't change. It is usually a straight line. In contrast, in Western emoticons, the symbols for the mouth change to show happiness and sadness.*

   b. Do all emoticons that indicate happiness use the same symbol for the mouth? _____

B Compare answers to Exercise A with a partner.

VOCABULARY PRACTICE

Academic Vocabulary

A Find the words in bold in Reading 1. Use the context to help you match each word to the correct definition.

_____ **1. reaction** (Par. 1)   **a.** look at something closely

_____ **2. category** (Par. 2)   **b.** societies that are similar in their way of life

_____ **3. cultures** (Par. 3)   **c.** works well and produces the intended results

_____ **4. focus** (Par. 4)   **d.** group of things that are similar

_____ **5. interpret** (Par. 5)   **e.** decide on a specific meaning or significance

_____ **6. effective** (Par. 6)   **f.** something you feel, say, or do because of something else

B Read the following sentences and choose the best phrase to complete each one.

1. The students all had a _____ to the teacher's announcement. They were delighted to go on a field trip.
   a. positive reaction   **b.** new reaction

2. A good photo can be a _____ way to communicate a complicated idea.
   a. highly effective   **b.** simply effective

3. Many _____ celebrated the New Year, too. For example, the Egyptians celebrated the "Opening of the Year" festival in mid-July.
   a. new cultures   **b.** ancient cultures

4. Public speakers often _____ just one person in the audience when they give a presentation. It can help them feel less nervous.
   a. focus on   **b.** focus in

5. One _____ fiction that is very popular right now is graphic novels.
   a. category on   **b.** category of

6. Researchers _____ after collecting the participants' answers to the questionnaire.
   a. interpret the results   **b.** interpret the analysis

Multiword Vocabulary

A Find the multiword vocabulary in bold in Reading 1. Use the context to help you understand the meaning. Then match each item to the correct definition.

_____ **1. facial expressions** (Par. 1)   **a.** looks identical but is the reverse of something

_____ **2. no matter whether** (Par. 2)   **b.** not depending on one thing or another

_____ **3. wide open** (Par. 2)   **c.** open to the maximum extent

_____ **4. is the mirror image of** (Par. 3) **d.** concentrate on

_____ **5. pay attention to** (Par. 5)   **e.** the ways your features move to communicate

_____ **6. in turn** (Par. 6)   **f.** in sequence or order

B Complete the following paragraph with the correct multiword vocabulary from Exercise A.

Last month, we moved into a new apartment in my building. Every floor has two apartments and each one _____ the other. We only moved because we
₁
thought this apartment was quieter than our other apartment, but, as it turns out, we were very wrong. The neighbor next door makes noise at all times of the day. He plays music very loudly _____ it is the middle of the night or 5:00 in the morning. He
₂
leaves his doors and windows _____, which makes it even
₃
noisier. He just doesn't seem to care about anyone but himself. You can tell by his _____ that he certainly doesn't
₄
_____ the needs of his neighbors! So, the other day, we decided
₅
to show him how it feels to have a bad neighbor. We started leaving our smelly garbage in the hall in front of his apartment. Our next-door neighbor, _____,
₆
started doing the same thing. He didn't care. The hallway got so smelly, it was obvious to everyone. Finally, he moved out! Problem solved.

Use the Vocabulary

Write answers to the following questions. Use the words in bold in your answers. Then share your answers with a partner.

1. What events in the news do you **pay attention to**? Why?

2. What would be your **reaction** if a friend needed to borrow money? How about if someone wanted you to help him cheat on a test?

3. What is something you do that you are particularly **effective** at?

4. What is one example of a behavior in your **culture** that is different in another **culture**?

5. Do you know someone who makes an unusual or interesting **facial expression**? Describe it.

THINK AND DISCUSS

Work in a small group. Use the information in the reading and your own ideas to discuss the following questions.

1. **Relate to personal experience.** Think of someone you know well. What part of the face does this person use the most to express him- or herself?

2. **Relate to personal experience.** Has someone ever looked at your face and thought you were angry, happy, or sad when you weren't? Have you looked at someone's face and made a similar mistake? What happened?

3. **Apply knowledge.** What do you think would be a good way to avoid miscommunication with someone from a different culture?

Academic Vocabulary

to adjust	partial	to reduce
to assume	positive	

Multiword Vocabulary

according to	to make the best of
to be easy to see	to put someone at ease
blood pressure	quality of life

Reading Preview

A **Preview.** Skim Reading 2 by reading the first and last sentence of each paragraph. Then check (✓) three topics below that you think might be in this reading.

_____ **1.** What social scientists do

_____ **2.** Why we smile

_____ **3.** Sayings about smiling

_____ **4.** Benefits of smiling

_____ **5.** Studies about smiling

_____ **6.** How to have a happier life

B **Topic vocabulary.** The following words appear in Reading 2. Look at the words and answer the questions with a partner.

analysis	feel-good	measuring
benefits	happier	stress
conflict	healthier	study
embarrassment		

1. Which words suggest that the reading will include scientific research?

2. Which words relate to negative feelings or situations?

3. Which words have to do with living well?

C **Predict.** What do you think this reading will be about? Discuss each word in Exercise B and predict how it may relate to the reading.

Smiles do much more than just communicate happiness. Read about the unexpected benefits of smiling, and learn when a smile is more than just a smile.

Portrait of a young girl smiling in Kumari, Nepal

The Science of Smiles

Why do we smile? Many people auto- 1
matically assume that there is a
simple answer to that question—we
smile because we are happy. That answer is
correct, but it doesn't tell the whole story. Social
scientists who study smiles say there's a lot more
to smiling than just showing happiness. Smiling
can actually have a great impact on a person's
quality of life.

Marianne LaFrance is a social scientist 2
who is particularly interested in smiles. She
has studied smiles for over 20 years. LaFrance
says that we use smiles to make and maintain
relationships. We need to do this because we are
social animals. As social animals, we need strong
relationships in order to survive and thrive.[1]
According to LaFrance, smiling is one of the most
important tools to maintain social relationships.
For example, smiling makes it easier to make
new friends. One reason for this is that we are
attracted to people who smile. Smiling can put
people at ease. Smiling also helps people make
the best of unexpected conditions and adjust to

difficult social situations. A smile can help reduce
conflict and ease embarrassment. In many lan-
guages, there are sayings that express the social
importance of smiling. For example, in English,
people say, "Smile and the whole world smiles
with you. Cry and you cry alone."

Smiling does more than just help us make 3
and maintain relationships, however. It seems
that the amount we smile and the quality of our

MORE FACTS ABOUT SMILES

- Babies smile inside their mothers before they are born.
- Not only do women smile more than men, but women have larger smile muscles than men.
- People who are guilty of some wrongdoing such as cheating on an exam are more likely not to be punished if they smile when they are caught.
- People who smile shortly after the death of a loved one, such as a husband or a wife, adjust more quickly to the loss than those who don't smile.

---

[1] *thrive:* do well and be successful, healthy, and strong

smiles may have some connection to our quality of life. Two studies show the relationship between smiling and the quality and length of people's lives. One study is the "Yearbook Study." In 2010, LeeAnne Harker and Dacher Keltner, two social scientists from the University of California, Berkeley, compared the lives of women they found in a thirty-year-old yearbook.[2] They rated the women's smiles by measuring the amount of muscle movement around the mouth and eyes. Then they asked the women to answer some questions about their lives. The results of their analysis showed that the women with the highest rated smiles in the pictures reported happier lives and happier and longer marriages.

"Social scientists who study smiles say there's a lot more to smiling than just showing happiness."

Another study is the "Baseball Card Study" from 2010. Ernest Abel and Michael Kruger from Wayne State University in Detroit, Michigan, found that the quality of the smile in pictures of baseball players could actually predict how long they would live. Abel and Kruger also rated the players' smiles. The rating system had three levels: no smile, partial smile, or full smile. They found that the players with full smiles lived approximately[3] seven years longer than the players pictured with partial smiles or with no smiles.

Research shows that smiling has many positive effects on our health. This might explain why the people in the studies with bigger smiles had longer lives. Studies show that smiling reduces stress and stress-related hormones.[4] It also lowers blood pressure. Smiling can affect the brain in the same way as exercise. For example, it increases the amount of feel-good hormones such as serotonin and endorphins. Endorphins not only make us feel better, but reduce pain as well. Furthermore, recent brain research shows that just the act of smiling can actually make us happier. In other words, we smile because something happens that makes us happy. But then, our smiles send a message back to the brain that makes us feel even happier.

Smiling is clearly good for us. We can even get the benefits of smiling just by making ourselves smile. One way to do this is to look at a picture of other people smiling. This is because smiling is contagious.[5] It is very difficult to look at others smiling and not smile back. Even thinking about people smiling can make you smile. It is easy to see that smiling is much more than just an expression of happiness. It's a powerful tool for maintaining both emotional and physical health.

---

[2] *yearbook:* a book containing photos and other information that celebrates the previous year at a school or college

[3] *approximately:* about the same as

[4] *hormones:* chemicals naturally occuring in your body

[5] *contagious:* able to spread to other people, such as a disease

READING COMPREHENSION

Big Picture

Ⓐ The following statements are the main ideas of some of the paragraphs in Reading 2. Write the correct paragraph number next to its main idea.

_____ **1.** A study of baseball players' smiles showed the connection between smiles and longer life.

_____ **2.** The work of a social scientist shows the role of smiling in maintaining relationships.

_____ **3.** Some research shows how the body benefits from smiling.

_____ **4.** A study of female students' smiles indicated their future happiness.

B Compare answers to Exercise A with a partner. Then complete the following sentence.

The main idea of the *whole* reading is that smiling has an important role in maintaining

_____ and _____ health.

Close-Up

A Decide which of the following statements are true or false according to Reading 2 and the short extra reading, "More Facts About Smiles," on page 178. Write *T* (True) or *F* (False) next to each one.

_____ **1.** LaFrance thinks that smiling is one of the most important social tools.

_____ **2.** In the "Yearbook Study," scientists measured the smiles of women in yearbooks.

_____ **3.** In the "Baseball Card Study," researchers connected the quality of smiles with how happy a person's marriage was.

_____ **4.** Researchers found that baseball players with partial smiles lived approximately seven years longer than players with full smiles.

_____ **5.** Scientists think there is a connection between smiling and long life.

_____ **6.** Serotonin helps reduce pain.

_____ **7.** If you see someone smile, it often makes you want to smile, too.

_____ **8.** Babies are born with the ability to smile.

_____ **9.** Men have larger smile muscles than women.

B Work with a partner or in a small group. Change the false statements in Exercise A to make them true.

Reading Skill

Understanding Reference Words

In Unit 5, you saw that writers use pronouns to refer to ideas that they already mentioned. Writers use other reference words, too, such as *this* (+ noun), *that* (+ noun), *these* (+ noun), and *those* (+ noun). Good readers know which piece of information the reference word refers to.

Examples:

People in different cultures smile for different reasons. This may be why people interpret emoticons differently.

In this sentence, "this" refers to the fact that people in different cultures smile for different reasons.

In the "Baseball Card Study," researchers looked at smiles of baseball players. Like the yearbook study, this study looked at how people smiled in photos.

In this sentence, "this" refers to the "Baseball Card Study."

A Find the following pairs of sentences from Reading 2. Circle the ideas that the underlined reference words refer to. The first one is done for you.

1. (Why do we smile?) Many people automatically assume there is a simple answer to that question. (Par. 1)

2. We smile because we are happy. That answer is correct, but it doesn't tell the whole story. (Par. 1)

3. LaFrance says that we use smiles to make and maintain relationships. We need to do this because we are social animals. (Par. 2)

4. For example, smiling makes it easier to make new friends. One reason for this is that we are attracted to people who smile. (Par. 2)

5. Research shows that smiling impacts our health positively in a variety of ways. This might explain why the people in the studies with bigger smiles had longer lives. (Par. 5)

6. We can even get the benefits of smiling just by making ourselves smile. One way to do this is to look at a picture of other people smiling. (Par. 6)

B Find the reference words in each of the following sets of sentences. Underline them. Work with a partner to decide what each reference word refers to.

1. LaFrance argues that humans are social animals. This means that they need strong relationships with other people in order to survive.

2. LaFrance observed that adolescent girls in North America are often told to smile more. On the other hand, North American male adolescents smile less because they are practicing being "cool"—unemotional. This is supported by one of LaFrance's studies.

3. Studies have also shown that men are less likely than women to return a smile when someone smiles at them. One explanation for this is hormones.

VOCABULARY PRACTICE

Academic Vocabulary

(A) Find the words in the box below in Reading 2. Use the context to help you choose the correct word to complete each of the following sentences.

> assume (Par. 1)   adjust (Par. 2)   reduce (Par. 2)   partial (Par. 4)   positive (Par. 5)

1. Having strong relationships with other people has many _____ effects on human health. For example, one benefit is that friendships can help people avoid depression.

2. One way to _____ stress in a situation is to tell a joke. People often feel less stressed when they laugh.

3. People _____ that being healthy is only about good diet and exercise. Actually, simple things such as smiling can keep us healthy, too.

4. Studies show that people _____ more quickly to major changes in their lives when they smile.

5. The researchers couldn't use any photos with _____ images of people's heads. They needed pictures that showed the entire face.

(B) Match the words in bold to words that they combine with in Reading 2. Write the letter on the line.

_____ **1. reduce**   **a. adjust**

_____ **2.** automatically   **b.** effects

_____ **3.** quickly   **c. assume**

_____ **4. partial**   **d.** smile

_____ **5. positive**   **e.** conflict

(C) Look at your answers in Exercise B. Write each phrase from Exercise B on the line opposite its definition below.

1. beneficial impacts   _____

2. make disagreements less big   _____

3. believe, without thinking, something is true   _____

4. become quickly used to a situation   _____

5. a facial expression that is not completely visible _____

Multiword Vocabulary

(A) Find the words in bold in Reading 2. Then write the words that come before and/or after them to complete the multiword vocabulary.

1. **quality of** _____ (Par. 1)

2. **According** _____ (Par. 2)

3. **put** people _____ **ease** (Par. 2)

4. make the _____ _____ (Par. 2)

5. _____ **pressure** (Par. 5)

6. is _____ **to** _____ (Par. 6)

B Complete the following sentences with the correct multiword vocabulary from Exercise A.

1. Money doesn't necessarily ensure a good _____ ; however, most people need friends and good health in order to enjoy life.

2. _____ Marianne LaFrance, people smile for different reasons in different cultures.

3. High _____ is a health risk. Losing weight may improve this condition because having a lower weight puts less stress on your heart.

4. Having a boring job can be unpleasant. To _____ the situation, ask your boss for more challenging responsibilities.

5. Doctors often can _____ patients _____ by explaining procedures in simple terms. Knowing what is going to happen makes most people feel less nervous.

6. Exercise increases endorphins, so it _____ that physical activity can improve a person's mood.

Use the Vocabulary

Write answers to the following questions. Use the words in bold in your answers. Then share your answers with a partner.

1. Have you ever had to **adjust** to a difficult situation? Explain your answer.
2. Do you or anyone in your family suffer from high **blood pressure**? Explain your answer.
3. Do you know of any ways to **reduce** high blood pressure? Explain your answer.
4. What conditions lead to a good **quality of life**?
5. Do you have any techniques for **putting** people **at ease**? What are they?
6. Can thinking **positive** thoughts improve a person's mood? Why, or why not?

THINK AND DISCUSS

Work in a small group. Use the information in the reading and your own ideas to discuss the following questions.

1. **Analyze.** What are some reasons for smiling that are not discussed in the reading passage?
2. **Relate to personal experience.** Do you smile much? If so, do you think it affects your physical or mental health?
3. **Evaluate.** What do you think of the "Yearbook Study" described in paragraph 3 of Reading 2? Do you think it is a good study? Why, or why not?

Vocabulary Review

A Complete the paragraphs with the vocabulary below that you have studied in the unit.

| according to | facial expressions | highly effective | puts us at ease |
| categories of | helps reduce | in turn | quickly adjust |

Being able to interpret _____ 1 is important to most people. Knowing what other people are thinking and feeling _____ 2 . It helps us decide if other people are trustworthy, and it _____ 3 tension. But understanding facial expressions can be complex. This is because there are at least two major _____ 4 facial expressions, _____ 5 some experts. These are *macroexpressions* and *microexpressions*. Macroexpressions are expressions that are easy to see such as smiles because they last for several seconds. An example of a microexpression is a blink. Microexpressions are much more difficult to notice because they last less than a half a second. Microexpressions often occur when people are trying to hide their feelings. Moreover, they are involuntary—people cannot control them.

Correctly interpreting microexpressions is a crucial part of some jobs such as police work and counseling. For example, police officers can change their method of questioning and _____ 6 if they know a suspect is lying. Counselors, _____ 7 , can prescribe better treatments when they know their clients' true feelings. Several experts have developed systems for training people to interpret microexpressions. These courses are _____ 8 . Among others, psychologists and animators have found the training to be useful in their work.

B Compare answers to Exercise A with a partner. Then discuss the following question.

How can successfully interpreting microexpressions help people?

C Complete the following sentences in a way that shows that you understand the meaning of the words in bold.

1. When I am talking to someone, I usually **focus on** his or her _____ .

2. When someone smiles at me, I **assume that** _____ .

3. When I meet someone new, I think it's important to **pay attention to** _____.

4. You can often **make the best of** a bad situation by _____.

D Work with a partner and write four sentences that include any four of the vocabulary items below.

to be easy to see	a new culture	a positive reaction
interpret results	a partial smile	quality of life

Connect the Readings

A Look back at Readings 1 and 2 to answer the questions in the chart below. Write notes in the boxes.

	Reading 1	Reading 2
1. What important fact did you learn in each reading?		
2. What is the purpose of making facial expressions?		
3. List the benefits of making the facial expressions discussed in Reading 1 and Reading 2.		
4. What aspects of smiles do the two readings discuss?		
5. What was the purpose of the research presented in each reading?		

B Compare answers to Exercise A with a partner or in a small group.

C Discuss the following questions with a partner. Use your understanding of the readings and your own ideas.

1. Can you imagine any changes you might make to your life as a result of knowing the benefits of smiling?

2. Are there cultural differences in the way people express doubt? How would you design a research study to find the answer to this question?

3. What are some benefits of accurately interpreting facial expressions?

VOCABULARY INDEX

The following words and phrases are studied in *Reading and Vocabulary Focus 2*. Each vocabulary item is listed according to which unit and reading it appears in. For example, a word or phrase listed as **U1 R1** appears in the first reading of unit 1. If a word is in the Academic Word List, it is listed as AWL.

a way of life   U7 R2
a wide range of   U7 R2
access (*n*) AWL   U4 R1, U7 R2
according to   U9 R2
adjust (*v*) AWL   U9 R2
affect (*v*) AWL   U5 R2
along with   U1 R2
analyze (*v*) AWL   U2 R2
anywhere in the world   U3 R1
area (*n*) AWL   U2 R2
art form (*n*)   U5 R1
assume (*v*) AWL   U9 R2
at any time   U4 R2
at one time   U5 R1
aware (*adj*) AWL   U2 R1
awareness (*n*) AWL   U7 R2

be addicted to   U4 R1
be better at   U5 R1
be concerned with   U2 R2
be easy to see   U9 R2
be in charge of   U6 R2
be made up of   U4 R2
be on the scene   U7 R1
be responsible for   U2 R1
be symbolic of   U3 R2
be the mirror image of   U9 R1
benefit (*n*) AWL   U2 R2
blood pressure (*n*)   U9 R2

category (*n*) AWL   U9 R1
challenging (*adj*)   U5 R1
city planning (*n*)   U3 R1
close together   U6 R2
code (*n*) AWL   U2 R2
come in (first, second, etc.)   U5 R2
come to the aid of   U7 R1
come to the conclusion that   U8 R1
committed (*adj*) AWL   U8 R2
community (*n*) AWL   U3 R1

compensation (*n*) AWL   U2 R1
complex (*adj*) AWL   U4 R1
conflict (*n*) AWL   U6 R2
considerably (*adv*) AWL   U2 R1
consist of (*v*)   U8 R1
constant (*adj*) AWL   U8 R1
construct (*v*) AWL   U3 R2
contact information (*n*)   U4 R2
contemporary (*adj*) AWL   U1 R1
convinced (*adj*) AWL   U7 R2
cooperate (*v*) AWL   U6 R1
coordination (*n*) AWL   U5 R1
culture (*n*) AWL   U9 R1

deprive(*v*)   U8 R1
design (*n*) AWL   U3 R2
determine (*v*)   U6 R1
device (*n*) AWL   U4 R2
distinctive (*adj*)   U3 R2
diverse (*adj*) AWL   U3 R2
do research on   U4 R2
dominant (*adj*) AWL   U6 R1
dramatic (*adj*) AWL   U6 R1
drive someone crazy   U8 R1

economic opportunities   U3 R1
effective (*adj*)   U9 R1
efficient (*adj*)   U4 R2
emerge from (*v*)   U8 R2
end up as   U1 R1
energy (*n*) AWL   U1 R2
enormous (*adj*) AWL   U7 R1
environment (*n*) AWL   U3 R1
evaluate (*v*) AWL   U7 R1
eventually (*adv*) AWL   U7 R2
expand (*v*) AWL   U4 R1
explore (*v*)   U1 R1
extend (*v*)   U4 R2

a facial expression   U9 R1

feature (*n*) AWL   U2 R2
focus (*v*) AWL   U9 R1
follow the rules   U6 R2
for the time being   U2 R1
from time to time   U6 R1
from up to [distance] away   U8 R2
function (*n*) AWL   U8 R2
furthermore (*adv*) AWL   U6 R2

get along with (*v*)   U6 R1
get something off the ground   U7 R2
grant (*n*) AWL   U1 R2

have a vision   U3 R2
have something in common   U4 R1
hold onto (*v*)   U1 R2

identify (*v*) AWL   U7 R1
identity theft (*n*)   U2 R2
illustrate (*v*) AWL   U4 R1
in place of   U1 R2
in search of   U6 R2
in some cases   U1 R2
in the meantime   U2 R2
in the process of   U2 R1
in turn   U9 R1
in use   U5 R1
incidence (*n*) AWL   U5 R2
income (*n*) AWL   U3 R2
injured (*adj*) AWL   U8 R2
instrument(*n*) AWL   U1 R1
intelligent (*adj*) AWL   U6 R2
interact (*v*) AWL   U4 R2
interaction (*n*) AWL   U6 R2
interfere with (*v*)   U8 R2
interpret (*v*) AWL   U9 R1
invasion of privacy   U2 R2

CREDITS

Text Sources

The following sources were consulted when writing the readings for *Reading and Vocabulary Focus 2*.

6–8: "The Vegetable Orchestra," http://www.vegetableorchestra.org/about.php; "15 Fascinating Food Artists and Sculptors," Webecoist: Going Beyond Green: http://webecoist.momtastic. com/2008/12/15/food-artists-and-sculptors/; "Mushrooms As Building Material For Architectural Structures And Furniture By Philip Ross," by Shana Ecker, Huffington Post: http://www. huffingtonpost.com/2012/10/01/mushrooms-as-building-material_n_1924370.html; "Forget Recycling: Here Comes Edible Packaging," by Paul Smith, Triple Pundit: People, Planet, Profit: http://www. triplepundit.com/2012/02/forget-recycling-comes-edible-packaging/; **16–17:** "The Wondrous Coconut," by Luna Shyr, NGM, March 2012; "Do Coconut Oil and Coconut Water Provide Health Benefits?" by Katherine Hobson and Angela Haupt, US News Health: http:// health.usnews.com/health-news/living-well-usn/articles/2012/03/06/do-coconut-oil-and-coconut-water-provide-health-benefits-2; **28–29:** "Babies Recognize Faces Better Than Adults, Study Says," by Hillary Mayell, National Geographic News: http://news.nationalgeographic.com/ news/2005/03/0321_050321_babies.html; "Brain Has 'Face Place' for Recognition, Monkey Study Confirms," by Anna Petherick, National Geographic News: http://news.nationalgeographic. com/news/2006/02/0203_060203_brain_2.html; **36–37:** "How Facial Recognition Systems Work," by Kevin Bonsor and Ryan Johnson, How Stuff Works: http://electronics.howstuffworks.com/ gadgets/high-tech-gadgets/facial-recognition.htm; **48–49:** "Urban Planning," by Mary Schons, National Geographic Education: http://education.nationalgeographic.com/education/news/ urban-planning/?ar_a=1; **56–57:** "Tomorrowland," by John Lancaster, National Geographic Magazine: http://ngm.nationalgeographic.com/2012/02/astana/lancaster-text; **68–69:** "Revealed World," by Tim Folger, National Geographic Magazine: http://ngm.nationalgeographic.com/ big-idea/14/augmented-reality; **76–77:** "Amber Case, Cyborg Anthropologist," [no author], National Geographic Magazine: http://www.nationalgeographic.com/explorers/bios/amber-case/; **88–89:** "This is your brain on music," by Steven Fick and Elizabeth, Canadian Geographic Shilts: http://www.canadiangeographic.ca/magazine/jf06/alacarte.asp; **96–97:** "Songs Stick in Everyone's Head," By Daniel J. DeNoon, WebMD Health News: http://www.webmd.com/ mental-health/news/20030227/songs-stick-in-everyones-head; "Earworms: The Song Stuck in Your Head," by Emma Burns, Synapse: The Boston University Undergraduate Science Magazine: http://www.bu.edu/synapse/2011/11/27/earworms/; "What Goes in One Ear Does Not Come Out the Other," by BU Synapse, The Quad: http://buquad.com/2011/09/14/what-goes-in-one-ear-does-not-come-out-the-other/; **108–111:** "Greater Flamingo," NGM: http://animals. nationalgeographic.com/animals/birds/greater-flamingo/?source=A-to-Z; "Wolf," NGM: http:// animals.nationalgeographic.com/animals/mammals/wolf/?source=A-to-Z; "Spotted Hyena," NGM: http://animals.nationalgeographic.com/animals/mammals/hyena/?source=A-to-Z; "Langur Monkey," by Laurie Childree, Critters 360: Animal Facts and Resources: http://www. helium.com/items/1562695-langur-monkey; **118–119:** "The Genius of Swarms," by Peter Miller, NGM: http://ngm.nationalgeographic.com/2007/07/swarms/miller-text/1; **130–131:** "Tsunami Blogs Help Redefine News and Relief Effort," by Brian Handwerk, National Geographic News: http://news.nationalgeographic.com/news/2005/01/0126_050126_tv_tsunami_blogs. html; **138–139:** "Citizen Journalism in Kibera," posted by Marilyn Terrell, Intelligent Travel,

NGM: http://blogs.nationalgeographic.com/blogs/intelligenttravel/2009/10/citizen-journalism-in-kibera.html; **150–152:** "Pollution," National Geographic Encyclopedia: http://education. nationalgeographic.com/education/encyclopedia/pollution/?ar_a=1; "Noise Pollution," U.S. Environmental Protection Agency: Air and Radiation: http://www.epa.gov/air/noise. html; "Marine Pollution," NGM: http://ocean.nationalgeographic.com/ocean/critical-issues-marine-pollution/; **158–159:** "Our Vanishing Night," by Verlyn Klinkenborg, NGM: http:// ngm.nationalgeographic.com/2008/11/light-pollution/klinkenborg-text; **170–171:** "Culture Is Key To Interpreting Facial Emotions," Science Daily: http://www.sciencedaily.com/ releases/2007/04/070404162321.htm; "Perception of Facial Expressions Differs Across Cultures," Science Daily: http://www.sciencedaily.com/releases/2011/09/110901105510.htm; "Fearful facial expressions enhance our perception," by Ed Yong, NGM: http://phenomena.nationalgeographic. com/2008/06/15/fearful-facial-expressions-enhance-our-perception/; **178–179:** "The Science of Unmasking Our Smiles!" by Kike Calvo, NGM News Watch: http://newswatch. nationalgeographic.com/2013/01/25/smile-the-science-behind-facial-expressions/; "An interview with Marianne LaFrance," by Anna Lena Phillips, American Scientist: http://www. americanscientist.org/bookshelf/pub/an-interview-with-marianne-lafrance

Art Credits

Cover: Greg Dale/National Geographic Creative; **iii:** (t) FRANS LANTING/National Geographic Creative; **iii:** (c) PAUL CHESLEY/National Geographic Creative; **iii:** (b) XPACIFICA/National Geographic Creative; **iv:** (t) Frank Rothe/Stone/Getty Images; **iv:** (c) REZA/National Geographic Creative; **iv:** (b) FRANS LANTING/National Geographic Creative; **v:** (t) MAYNARD OWEN WILLIAMS/National Geographic Creative; **v:** (c) SAIFULLIZAN DAINI/National Geographic Creative; **v:** (b) mauritius images GmbH/Alamy; **vi:** (t) Frank Rothe/Stone/Getty Images; **vi:** (b) Lev Dolgachov/Alamy; **vii:** Oliver Uberti/National Geographic Magazine Staff; **ix:** Matthew Richardson/Alamy; **2–3:** FRANS LANTING/National Geographic Creative; **4–5:** Cathy Scola/Flickr Open/Getty Images; **6–7:** PATRICK BERNARD/AFP/Getty Images; **7:** The Art Archive at Art Resource, NY; **8:** JOEL SARTORE/National Geographic Creative; **10:** JOEL SARTORE/National Geographic Creative; **13:** PATRICK BERNARD/AFP/Getty Images; **14–15:** ROBIN MOORE/National Geographic Creative; **16–17:** MIKE THEISS/National Geographic Creative; **16:** (br) MARK THIESSEN/National Geographic Creative; **22:** (bl) DigiPub/Flickr/Getty Images; **22:** (bc) Paul Edmondson/Mint Images RF/Getty Images; **22:** (br) Thomas Flügge/E+/Getty Images; **24–25:** PAUL CHESLEY/National Geographic Creative; **26–27:** ALEX TREADWAY/National Geographic Creative; **28–29:** Andrey Burmakin/Fotolia LLC; **31:** Roy Lawe/Alamy; **32:** EDHAR/Shutterstock.com; **34–35:** Peter Arnold/Stegerphoto/Getty Images; **36:** (t) KIMIHIRO HOSHINO/AFP/Getty Images/Newscom; **36:** (br) Franck Boston/Fotolia LLC; **41:** Ian Waldie/Staff/Getty Images News/Getty Images; **42:** MICHAEL NICHOLS/National Geographic Creative; **44–45:** XPACIFICA/National Geographic Creative; **46–47:** JIM RICHARDSON/National Geographic Creative; **48–49:** Gavin Hellier/Robert Harding World Imagery/Getty Images; **54–55:** ibrahimusta/iStock/Thinkstock; **56:** Jane Sweeney/The Image Bank/Getty Images; **57:** JEROME COOKSON/National Geographic Creative; **61:** Jane Sweeney/Lonely Planet Images/Getty Images; **62–63:** fotoVoyager/E+/Getty Images; **64–65:** Frank Rothe/Stone/Getty Images; **66–67:** Lev Dolgachov/Alamy; **68–69:** Oliver Uberti/National Geographic Magazine Staff; **74–75:** MARK THIESSEN/National Geographic Creative; **76:** Hutton Supancic/WireImage/Getty Images; **77:** REUTERS/Eloy Alonso (SPAIN BUSINESS SOCIETY SCI TECH); **82:** Matthew Richardson/Alamy; **84–85:** REZA/National Geographic Creative; **86–87:** JOHN SCOFIELD/National Geographic Creative; **88:** Custom Medical Stock Photo; **94–95:** KAREN KASMAUSKI/National Geographic Creative; **96:** Lebrecht Music and Arts Photo Library/Alamy; **97:** Dorling Kindersley/Getty Images; **102:** Hill Street Studios/Blend Images/Getty Images; **104–105:** FRANS LANTING/National Geographic Creative; **106–107:** KLAUS NIGGE/National Geographic Creative; **108:** JOEL SARTORE/National Geographic Creative; **109:** JIM AND JAMIE DUTCHER/National Geographic Creative; **110:** FRANS LANTING/National Geographic Creative; **111:** Christian Kober/AWL Images/Getty Images; **116–117:** HENRY JAGER/National Geographic Creative; **118:** Christoph Burki/The Image Bank/Getty Images; **123:** F1online digitale Bildagentur GmbH/Alamy; **124:** FRANS LANTING/National Geographic Creative; **126–127:** MAYNARD OWEN WILLIAMS/National Geographic Creative; **128–129:** Manuel Silvestri/Reuters; **130–131:** AFP/Getty Images; **131:** Bettman/Corbis; **132:** Tom Williams/Roll Call/Newscom; **135:** Paula Bronstein/Getty Images; **136–137:** John Warburton-Lee Photography/Alamy; **138–139:** SIMON MAINA/AFP/Getty Images; **143:** Jerome Starkey/Flickr Vision/Getty Images; **144:** CESAR MANSO/AFP/Getty Images; **146–147:** SAIFULLIZAN DAINI/National Geographic Creative; **148–149:** Asad Malik/Flickr Vision/Getty Images; **150–151:** STEFAN